The Earth is a Spaceship

By the same author:

THE CURSE OF THE AZTEC DUMMY: A Nebraskan Chronicle
IS THE MOON THE CENTER OF THE UNIVERSE?
HISTORY OF RUSSIA & THE SOVIET UNION in Humorous Verse
MAKE MARZIPAN, NOT WAR: Crazy Rhymes for Crazy Times
CHEESE PIRATES: Humorous Rhymes for Adult Children
CAFÉ BOMBSHELL: The International Brain Surgery Conspiracy
PETS OF THE GREAT DICTATORS & Other Works

See excerpts at www.newacademia.com

The Earth is a Spaceship

Sabrina Ramet's wackiest, wittiest, and wildest verses

Washington, DC

Copyright © 2020 by Sabrina P. Ramet

New Academia Publishing, 2020

All rights reserved. No part of this book may be reproduced or transmitted in any form or by any means, electronic or mechanical, including photocopying, recording, or by any information storage and retrieval system.

Printed in the United States of America

Library of Congress Control Number: 2019918391
ISBN 978-1-7326988-8-8 paperback (alk. paper)

 An imprint of new Academia Publishing
4401-A Connecticut Ave. NW, #236, Washington DC 20008

 info@newacademia.com
www.newacademia.com

For Kemal Hadžijusufović

Preface	xi
World history from ancient times to 1917	1
Gallia est omnis divisa	2
Caligula's horse	4
Onward, Leif!	5
Church-run brothels	6
Baldwin XVIII	7
Suleyman and his gazehounds go to Vienna for dinner	8
The Mayan Calendar	9
Joanna the Nutty	11
Ivan the Terrible and his terrible goldfish	12
The King is mad	13
Fyodor the bell-ringer	16
Oliver Cromwell on his elephant	18
Ekaterina, you're so great	20
C'é la Marx	22
Twentieth-Century political figures	23
You cannot be right against the party, or Trotsky agreed with himself	24
Qaddafi's sweet-scented camel	26
Ceauşescu's monkeys	28
Mao's cockroach	29
Kim Il Sung's fellow traveler	31
You are old, Comrade Brezhnev, and so is your hawk	33
Gierek the leader & Melsor the toad	35
Mobuto's pig	37

Enver, don't shoot!	39
Saparmurat Niazov Turkmenbashi's orchard of unicorns	41
Welcome in Libya	43
Die gute Zeiten rollen lassen	44

Religion — 47
Were Adam and Eve really married?	48
The meals of Friar Aquinotle	50
Chorus of the Holy Fathers	52
In heaven, the saints eat tomatoes	54
He earned indulgence, yes!	56
In the confessional	57
O mamma, are you a virgin?	60

Philosophical ruminations — 61
Tea with Aunt Mabel	62
Machiavelli on the streets of Firenze	64
Spinoza	66
Taxidermy daddy (Jeremy Benthan)	67
Dancing Mind-to-Mind (Georg Wilhelm Friedrich Hegel)	69
Salvation through Hegel	70
That's Bakunin	71
Wie einst, Platon-Liebling	72
In Friedrich Nietzsche's brain	74

Americana — 75
A message from the Minnesota tourist bureau	76
Seventeen cowboys	78
William Walker, King of Nicaragua	79
Warren G. Harding's teapot	82
J. Edgar Hoover's coming to town	84
If the mayor were a pigeon	86
At the polls	87
Stopgap, Kansas	88

The animal world   89
    Possible rabbits in this house   90
    All aboard, kitties!   91
    Lions and tigers   93
    Who let the ants come in?   94
    Do crocodiles have ghosts?   96
    The mystery of feline reproduction   98

Literature, language, reggae   99
    Ba-ba-daah   100
    Reggae archaeologicae   101
    Oh, Shakespeare was a poet   103
    Tribute to Edgar Allan Poe – may he forgive me   105
    I speak Splat   107
    Great Classics summarized in verse   108
    Christopher Marlowe and his work   110
    A girl named Lapuca   111
    On Dumpledy-Down   112
    Alice in Limerickland   113
    Ode to the semicolon;   118

Ordinary life   121
    The whole world's an ashtray   122
    Building without mold   123
    Utensils   125
    Something in my nose   126
    Derry down down down derry down   127
    Where is my wandering robot now?   128
    Pizza crisis   130
    Naked Airlines   132
    Porridge in tins   133
    Father Christmas and Mr. Holly   135
    Sayings, or The Adventures of Mick and Butch,   137
    Part Two
    Gourmette cuisine (oh, you wanted gourmet   138
    dining?)
    My father told me   140

Yeah, happy brush!	141
Shampoo causes insanity	142
My neighbor worships my dog	143
A guide on how to riot	145
Rabbit Hood	146
The Lone Rabbit	147
Yo-ho yo, a professor's life for me	148
Thick rubber membrane	149
Mental, dental, & physical health	**151**
The secret of long life	152
Colonoscopy	153
Haircuts in Honolulu	154
Song of the happy brain surgeons	156
Should I be concerned?	158
There's a rabbit in my brain	159
O Tannlege	160
Dental work in Tijuana (another Christmas song)	162
Outer spaces, local bases, foreign places	**163**
Best toilets in the galaxy	164
Alien implant	165
Home, sweet home	166
Forward brothers!	167
Oh, sociology, don't you cry for me	168
Bring back my Bonnie to me – zombie version	169
Welcome in our hotel!	170
I'm gonna sail to Liechtenstein	172
Hotel Gabrovo (International Joke Capital of the World, and of Europe)	174
The Earth is a spaceship	176

Preface

During the years 2001-2019, I composed approximately 450 mostly humorous verses; all but two of the verses included herein were published by New Academia Publishing in the following books: *Pets of the Great Dictators & other works* (2006), *Cheese Pirates: Humorous Rhymes for Adult Children* (2011), *Make Marzipan, Not War: Crazy rhymes for crazy times* (2013), *History of Russia & the Soviet Union in Humorous Verse* (2014), and *Is the Moon the Center of the Universe? A Reassessment of Many Things in Humorous Verse* (2016). I have selected roughly 100 of my favorites for inclusion in this collection. I am grateful to my sweetie and life partner, Christine Marie Hassenstab, for her enthusiasm for my rhyming and for joining me, together with Thomas Berker, Sophus Hvasshovd and Salahedin Vahabpoor, in performing some of my verses at the bookshop of the Norwegian University of Science & Technology, and for joining me several times with Zach Irwin, Jerry Pankhurst, Francine Friedman, and Mills Kelly, in performing some of these verses at annual conventions of the American Association for the Advancement of Slavic Studies, later renamed the Association for Slavic, East European, and Eurasian Studies. I also took part in public performances of some of my verses in Tartu, Estonia, with Jerry Pankhurst, Alar Kalp, Laura Roop, and Tom Hashimoto, and in Zagreb, Croatia, with Leonina Lončar, Arno Vinković, and Zvonimir Prusina, as well as a local choir led by Petru Marušić. I am also deeply grateful to Anna Lawton, my publisher, for her enthusiasm for my work, and to Andrew Cannon, who first encouraged me to pursue a career as a writer of verse.

Sabrina P. Ramet
Saksvik, September 2019

WORLD HISTORY
FROM ANCIENT TIMES TO 1917

Gallia est omnis divisa

Julius Caesar knew that Gaul
had three provinces in all,
He knew they differed just a bit,
in laws and customs and clothes that fit.
He gave speeches people liked,
From miles around the people hiked
just to hear the Roman Caesar,
He was such a people pleaser.

He knew that on the floor of life,
were none as lovely as his wife,
Unless it was his mistress
Or Cleopatra, second wife.
The ship of sails, it was so big,
It tasted like a sun-baked fig,
He shared the feast with friends and foes
But made them pirouette upon their toes.

He served up banquets in his suite,
He said he wanted friends to eat,
so that they would end up fat,
and pleased in Caesar's habitat.
He gave speeches people liked,
From miles around the people hiked
just to hear the Roman Caesar,
He was such a people pleaser.

He brought Britain under Rome,
his enemies should dress in foam,
so they could be recognized
and that he would not be surprised.
But on the Ides of March a group
of men in togas on the stoop
drew their blades and pressed their best
to draw royal blood from Caesar's chest.

So when you listen what you hear
and in your brain you hear it clear,
that Caesar wanted to be King,
Well maybe there's another thing.
Because on life are many factors,
Many roles and many actors,
Which is which is known to some,
But thinking can be cumbersome.

Upon the floor of life you find,
Plastic pigeons of a kind
that you cannot eat or feed,
Or your face on Caesar's coin you need.
But Rome, it fell – and thus to fellows,
Whose intent was aught but mellow.
Time, it's but, will not erase
the memories of in that place.

And if you think the syntax strange,
or grammar wandering off the range,
It is the meaning you should trod,
to see what's sense and what is odd.
Lest tidgets, mickles, fenesore,
Much too rorfad to ignore,
In the magic yatsoflage,
Here's a morbid haste of zage.

Caligula's Horse

Caligula sat on his horse
and sipped his chug-a-lug rum,
He motioned to his Celtic slave
who rapped his rat-a-tat drum.

Caligula thought he was grand
and rang for his ring-a-ding slaves.
He didn't trust his courtiers, no!
and sent them to toodle-doo graves.

But Caesar thought his horse was smart
and he liked his pitter-pat trot,
He promoted him to consul, yes!
But there was a peek-a-boo plot!

One night he took a perfumed bath
and enjoyed a rub-a-dub soak,
when the barons thinking him insane,
made sure that the big wig croaked.

Onward, Leif!

Old Leif Ericson, he was always well met,
attired in leather with a metal helmet.
"Onward, vikings!" he used to like to shout,
"Let's go find a continent, I think I know the route."
So, all his Vikings got aboard a lovely ship,
shouting out "hurray" and a very lively "yip!"
They docked in Greenland, got a little drunk,
worried 'bout the future and sank into a funk.
Then Old Leif Ericson pounded on his chest
and told his merry Vikings "Keep sailing to the West.
If we keep on sailing, we'll surely find that we
end up getting somewhere, wherever that may be."
And so they kept on sailing, fantasizing tuna,
'til their vessel entered into a laguna.
"It's Canada!" Leif bellowed and fell into a trance,
his happy Vikings broke into a dance.
Leif regained his consciousness – that was very brisk –
and told his crew that they should dine on ice-cold lutefisk.
They ate the fish and looked around and got back on their ship,
soon the crew was homeward bound, finished with their trip.
Ericson is famous, not so much his crew,
but everything I've told you here is absolutely true.

Church-run brothels

(In the 1300s and 1400s, Church-run brothels proliferated in Central Europe. A program on the History Channel attributed the initiative for this phenomenon to one Johann (John) of Salzburg, who believed that the brothels could encourage men to prefer sex with women over sex with other men, while, at the same time, helping to promote Christianity. The following verse offers some reflections on this theme. The verse is set to the music of "Happy days are here again", a song composed in 1929, with music by Milton Ager and lyrics by Jack Yellen.)

Church-run brothels in your town –
they banish sadness and your frown,
and the prostitutes discuss the faith:
happy brothels in your town.

John of Salzburg – he was smart –
he learned Church doctrines from a tart,
and he thought that was the way to start
a religious class for men.

He hoped as well that these whirls
would get men attracted to girls,
hey –

Church-run brothels are the rage,
and they provide a healthy stage
for long discussions of the faith –
happy brothels come of age!

Baldwin XVIII

Baldwin the 18th was such a persister,
married three women including his sister.
His sister was already wed to their uncle
who presented the newly weds with a carbuncle.
But uncle had two wives already it seems
and one was a man – the Bishop of Riems.
This uncle, whose name was Rodbert of Rhodes,
spent every Saturday reciting quaint odes.
His daughter was wed to the town's parish priest
and it's said that their sexual life never ceased.
But each of the two had a man on the side,
and the priest for his part always tested each bride.
And the parish priest's brother was really none other
than plaything to Rodbert of Rhodes' stepmother.
Locally known as Edwina the Rude,
she often paraded around in the nude.
The bishop approved, since he had a good view,
and rewarded Edwina with her personal pew.
Edwina once slept with the four altar boys --
it's said that they made an incredible noise,
and the boys, at Saint Schnitzler's, once had a fling
with Baldwin the 18th, their landsman and king.

Suleyman and his gazehounds go to Vienna for dinner

Suleyman was sultan and he was quite a guy,
Five-foot-six and wavy hair and sabers on each thigh.
He had a pack of gazehounds, they lived on roasted meat.
He'd trained them to do somersaults – now that was quite a feat.

And when he fancied schnitzel, he took his troops to Wien.
He laid siege to the city: his troops made quite a scene.
Yet with ropes and hooks and ladders, they couldn't scale the wall
But Suleyman liked coffee and the smell put all in thrall.

The Viennese sent word to him, "That smell is just magnificent,
And if you give us coffee, it would be so munificent."
So Suleyman decided to offer them a deal:
He would give them coffee, if they'd prepare a meal.

So everyone had schnitzel – his troops and caribou,
The eunuchs and the harem girls, and yes, the gazehounds too.
And when they had departed and gone back to whence they came,
The Viennese – they promised him an everlasting fame.

The Mayan Calendar

(May be sung to the tune of "Rawhide".)

Mayan Mayan Mayan
flyin' flyin' flyin'
from another planet to earth.
They must have had their reasons
to want to see our seasons,
they had a sense of humor and mirth.
Mayan Mayan Mayan
they were always cryin'
missin' the home they left behind.

Gonna end, count the days,
count the days, gonna end
gonna end, count the days
Ma-yan!
Calen-dar, what's it mean?
Why does it have an end?
When it ends, will we too?
Ride 'em in, Ma-yan!

Mayan Mayan Mayan
tryin' tryin' tryin'
wantin' to create so fast
a calendar for trackin'
the days that we are lackin'
for as long as earth would last.
Then they started packin'
made a fast back-trackin'
departed from their Yucatan home.

They were here, where'd they go?
Where'd they go, they were here.
They were here, where'd they go?
Ma-yan!
Did they know? Did they tell?
Did they tell? Did they know?
Did they know? Did they tell?
Ride 'em in, Mayan!

Joanna the Nutty

Joanna the Nutty was Queen of Castile,
nothing so pleased her as a venison meal,
except for her husband, Philip the Fair,
unless he was riding around on his mare.
She liked when he sat with her, stroking her hair,
but at least 20 ladies liked Philip the Fair.
So to Philip, it seemed only proper and right,
to divide his time equally, daytime and night,
between his betrothed and the ladies he knew,
who patiently waited all lined in a queue.
So handsome was Philip that all through the land,
locals would sing and strike up the band,
whenever he rode to their place of abode,
dismounted and then so boldly he strode.
Joanna and Philip – they knew many things,
such as why snakes and lizards do not have wings.
Joanna denied that the cosmos was boundless,
and considered that theory utterly groundless.
She wanted to demonstrate once and for all,
that the cosmos was bounded by a great granite wall.
Philip thought travel in time was a notion,
sure to provoke a happy commotion.
Some say he succeeded but just for a while,
and brought back some pizzas and served them in style.
Just look at the art and see for yourself,
How Philip kept pizzas lined on his shelf.
Now you have heard all about this royal pair,
'bout Joanna the Nutty and Philip the Fair.
If people should tell you that things were not so,
just tell them that you always know what you know.

Ivan the Terrible and his terrible goldfish

I've never seen a fish laugh,
at least not very loudly,
said Ivan the Terrible to himself,
as he gazed in the mirror proudly.

I've never seen a goldfish smile
Hey diddle diddle for the Oprichnina,
Maybe that's just not their style,
Hey diddle diddle for the Oprichnina.

My little fish must be a priest,
It likes to sing in chant.
But that terrible fish always sings off key --
which is why it must stay in the tank.

Bash them, smash them, and give them the lash,
Hey diddle diddle for the Oprichnina,
All of my enemies gonna crash,
Hey diddle diddle for the Oprichnina.

The King is Mad

After a pleasing midday repast,
King George the Third fancied an outing.
Although he had lost his lands in the West,
he had finally finished his pouting.
He clapped his hands twice and then shouted out,
"So let us be off, merry men.
Harness the horses and polish the carriage,
we'll drive to a close forest glen."

And so they took off with a rattley boom
and drove down a gravely road,
they passed an Old Hickory tree and a fence
and passed a small Mill House – we make no pretense.
An American sphinx they passed on the left,
a tippy canoe was tipped on the right.
They spied a red fox in wide field of poppies,
as a Kansas cyclone brought every delight.

King George, his royal personage, chatted away
to no one at all, but was feeling so cheery.
Then they came to a forest glen, barely in time,
for the horses were getting quite weary.
The King looked around, his eyes growing wide,
jumped out of the carriage and ran to a tree,
exclaiming quite joyfully, tipping his crown,
"Hey, Louis, you rotter, it's Georgie, it's me!"

Yes, Louis the Sixteenth was clearly in view,
just standing alone in the clime.
They could hear the soundtrack music so sweet,
as befitted two kings in their prime.
They chatted so amiably as two kings can do,
and exchanged many a joke,
but his driver and staff looked on quite aghast,
as the king conversed with an oak.

"King Louis" said:
"Faith is like a sparrow
that flies around for miles,
looking for a rooftop
to rest upon its tiles.
It flits around from place to place
and sometimes it is certain
that it has found just what it sought
like good old Thomas Merton."

To which, King George replied:
"I'm standing in a pudding,
a weasel is my cook.
I once sprang up a chimney
just to have a look.
But there was nothing much to see,
and so I went back down,
grabbed my scepter, donned my crown,
dressed up once more in royal gown."

But it was not King Louis at all, nor a fat imposter,
nor even mother or his dad,
but only an oak tree full with verdant leaves.
Yes, truly the king had gone mad –
yet, wise in his madness and mad in his wisdom:
some said he was even insane.
But we should be discreet and a little genteel,
for his majesty had a long reign.

Fyodor the bell-ringer

Fyodor Ivanovich, he was tsar,
he heard bells from near and far –
big bells, small bells, tiny little tinkle bells,
listened to bells in his boudoir.
With a ring-a-ding ding, and a ring-a-ding dong,
ring-a-ding, ring-a-dong all day long.

Policy-making was a bore:
he told his ministers to attend to that chore,
big bells, small bells, tiny little tinkle bells,
that was the sound he could adore.
With a ring-a-ding ding, and a ring-a-ding dong,
he liked to hear bells all day long.

Off to the chapel he would spring,
they had bells that he could ring:
big bells, small bells, tiny little tinkle bells,
did as he liked 'cause he was king.
With a ring-a-ding ding, and a ring-a-ding dong,
he could ring bells all day long.

Sometimes he would like to kneel,
his courtiers played the glockenspiel,
big bells, small bells, tiny little tinkle bells,
and back to bells with renewed zeal.
With a ring-a-ding ding, and a ring-a-ding dong,
ring-a-ding, ring-a-dong all day long.

Oliver Cromwell on his elephant

Oliver Cromwell – he had style
He could flash a winning smile,
He had won the Civil war
And if you wait I'll tell you more.

He had a *snake* called Rupert *Blake*
He had an alligator
He had a *steed* all dressed in *tweed*
He had a weasel-waiter.

He had a *plan* of things to *ban*
like *rum* and *ale* and *whiskey*
He had an Indian *elephant*
who *some*times could be *frisky*.

Oliver Cromwell – he had style
He could flash a winning smile,
He had won the Civil War
And if you wait I'll tell you more.

He found the time to *battle* crime
like *going* to the *pubs,*
There *shouldn't* be space for a horsey race,
There *shouldn't* be ticket *stubs!*

He *sits* on top of his elephant,
the Lord Protector's perch,
and keeps an eye on everyone
who's praying in the church.

Oliver Cromwell – he had style,
He could flash a winning smile,
He had won the Civil War
And if you wait I'll tell you more.

He couldn't wait to *regu*late
the *clothing* people wore.
All of his pets – they *had* no choice:
Why *should* the plebs have more?

If you reflect quite *circum*spect,
I *think* you may con*clude*
that *all* of the bans and *ban*ning plans
were *aimed* at what was *lewd* –

at *least* in the mind of *Crom*well,
a *mod*est man and *maybe*
who *wanted* to see each *citizen* free
of *sin* like a *new*born *baby*.

Oliver Cromwell – he had style,
He could flash a winning smile,
He had won the Civil War,
He had elephants galore!

Ring around the roundhead
Another round of tea,
I can hardly wait to drink
Another two or three.

Ekaterina, you're so great!

(Composed to the tune of "Der Trommelmann".)

Ekaterina – ja,
pa-rampa-pa-pa
she was the ruler – da,
pa-rampa-pa-pa
she had some lovers – si,
pa-rampa-pa-pa
she left them happy – yes,
pa-rampa-pa-pa, rampa-pa-pa, rampa-pa-pa.

She, the Empress – oui,
pa-rampa-pa-pa
she annexed Poland – po
pa-rampa-pa-pa,
but no, not all of it,
pa-rampa-pa-pa
she shared it with some friends
pa-rampa-pa-pa, rampa-pa-pa, rampa-pa-pa.

Now the whole world says,
pa-rampa-pa-pa
that she was really great
pa-rampa-pa-pa
and surely you agree
pa-rampa-pa-pa
and surely you agree,
pa-rampa-pa-pa, rampa-pa-pa, rampa-pa-pa,
Rampa-pa-pa!!

C'é la Marx

(Inspired, roughly, by the tune of "C'é la luna", a song popularized by Louis Prima)

No no no no, it never is too late,
no no no, to overthrow the state
no no no, 'cause it's capitalism's mate,
no no no, exploitation's not our fate.

Marx and Engels wanted more
and to open up the door
for a better life for workers,
Why give profits to the shirkers
just because they own the store?

No no no no, it never is too late,
no no no, to overthrow the state
no no no, 'cause it's capitalism's mate,
no no no, exploitation's not our fate.

Hey! the system's bad – alas!
Inequalities of class –
and they make our stomachs growl.
Exploitation is so foul
that I hope it cannot last,
I feel so alienated that I always gotta sing…

No no no no, it never is too late
no no no, to overthrow the state
no no no, 'cause it's capitalism's mate,
no no no, exploitation's not our fate!

TWENTIETH CENTURY POLITICAL FIGURES

You cannot be right against the party,
or
Trotsky agreed with himself

It's clear that if the party's right
and you don't agree
that you are clearly in the wrong
and don't think that you're free,
'cause freedom means that you are right
and not to be in error,
to choose to stay in ignorance
is self-inflicted terror.
You cannot be right
you cannot be right
against the party, no!

This insight came from Trotsky,
before he lost to Koba,
At least he didn't lose his teeth,
for that he thanked his zubar.
But once he'd lost to Stalin
ole Trotsky said the key
would be to make another party
with which he could agree.
You cannot be right
you cannot be right
against the party, no!

An International was what
was needed all around,
it would be number 4 because
the Third had run aground.

And if he ran the party, well,
he knew he would agree
with everything the party said,
the slogan would still be:
You cannot be right
you cannot be right
against the party, no!

Qaddafi's sweet-scented camel

Refrain: Slippery sluppery, slap slap slap,
Muammar al-Qaddafi on a camel's lap,
Qaddafi is taking a little nap.
Slippery sluppery slap slap slap.

Qaddafi dreams of love's sweet rapture,
lolling about in a field of toast,
and how he suavely set out to capture
the loveliest damsel on Libya's coast.

Repeat refrain.

The toast is ready for a buttering now,
Qaddafi spreads it nice and thick.
The damsel's heart is a-fluttering now,
lucky to be the leader's pick.

Repeat refrain.

Qaddafi sets the fashion's pace
attired in the finest silk.
The damsel feels her passions race
while she drinks a mug of camel's milk.

Repeat refrain.

He's bounded onto the camel's hump,
She's joined him on top of this mammal.

They're trotting off with a clippedy-clump
and feeding the toast to the camel.

Repeat refrain.

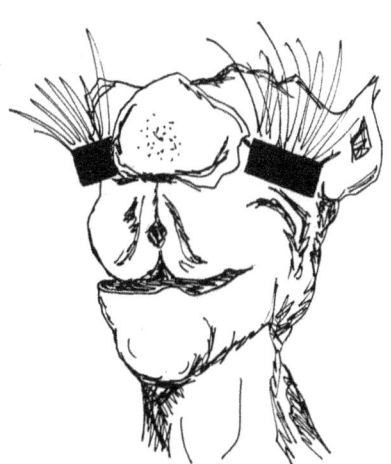

Ceauşescu's monkeys

'Twas the night before May Day
and all through the land
Not a comrade was stirring –
that's how it was planned.
The self-criticisms were laid
on the desktop with care,
in hopes that Ceauşescu
soon would be there.
But old Nick was soaring up high in the sky
his sleigh being pulled by a bevy of monkeys.
"Come Voitec, come Trofim, come Cornel Burtica,
Come Gheorghe Petrescu, come all of my flunkeys!"
I sat on my bed and heard such a commotion,
I figured it must be a purge or demotion.
And then there he was, that jolly old elf,
dressed in Bolshevik red, in spite of himself.
He unpacked his five-year plans right under my eye,
and then sprang up the chimney and took to the sky.
And as he flew by, I heard him exclaim,
"Whatever goes wrong, I don't take the blame."

Mao's cockroach

Mao Zedong
Great Leader of the Chinese people
Banned all pets!
Cultural Revolution,
he called it:
the Great Proletarian Cultural Revolution.

"Close the theaters, close the schools,
close the temples,
ban all operas (except "High Tide of Revolutionary
Fervor" and "The party – the people – a better future"),
ban all pets!
Ban all films (except for agitprop)
Long live the Working People of China!"

Mao didn't like pets.
But every night
when he went to the fridge for milk,
a small cockroach ran under the counter
a small cockroach Mao called "October,"
after the Great October Revolution.
October didn't like the light,
He liked it dark,
He kept out of sight
during the day.
Communism, capitalism – they all seemed the same,
thought October.

No matter what the system,
if you don't watch out,
somebody will step on you.

Kim Il Sung's fellow traveler

"No city is complete
without a giant gold statue of me,"
Kim il Sung once said
and he was right.
He put one up in P'yongyang --
that was a complete city.
It stood 300 feet in height,
from base to crown.
But few have noticed
that, under his golden arm,
the Great Noble Leader --
gold version --
is holding a small crocodile,
his fellow traveler.
Kim often said
that crocodiles were "forward-looking"
And he was right.
But there was more:
"Many persons will travel with us
along much of the path to communism,"
Kim il Sung once said,
echoing Stalin,
and he was right.
"They can be useful,
even if they will not travel with us
the whole distance."
And he was right.
A crocodile may not know much

about communism,
but he may be useful
all the same.
Kim Il Sung once said so,
or something to that effect;
it does not really matter exactly what he said,
what matters
is that he was right.
And I agree with him --
whatever he said,
because he was right.
His crocodile was less profound
And talked mainly about the menu.
He claimed that fish and birds and turtles
were the most flavorful,
And he was right.

You are old Comrade Brezhnev and so is your hawk

"You are old Comrade Brezhnev," the young pioneer said,
"and your muscles are no longer limber,
But you toss around logs as if they were nothing.
Pray how do you lift all this timber?"

"In my youth," said Leonid Ilych, "in the communist league,
I recited the Eighteenth Brumaire
For hours on end, 'til I had it by heart.
After that, logs seem lighter than air."

"You are old, Comrade Brezhnev," the young pioneer said,
"and you've grown most conspicuously fat,
But you locked up ten dissidents in five seconds flat.
Pray, sir, how can you manage that?"

"In my youth," said Leonid Ilych, "I'd often denounce
All the capitalists who tried to repress us.
I grew so adept that it's nothing at all
To imprison these scum who depress us."

"You are old, Comrade Brezhnev," the young pioneer said,
"And your mind is essentially dead.
Yet you've trained a pet hawk how to handle your car.
Pray, how did you manage to train her that far?"

"In my youth I commanded a squadron of tanks,"
said Leonid Ilych, improving the story.
"With my hawk at my side I defended my flanks

and pushed onward to triumph and glory.
Since then I have shared every trick of the trade
with my pet hawk who sits at my side.
So what's the surprise if after these years,
my hawk takes me out for a ride?"

"You are old, Comrade Brezhnev, and so is your hawk,
And all of the Politburo as well.
Yet your hawk's writing her memoirs and you've written yours.
Pray, why do you make our lives hell?"

"I have listened in patience to all of your prattle,
and have answered three questions of yours.
Now out of my sight or I'll throw you in jail
and I'll make sure to twice-bolt the doors."

Gierek the leader & Melsor the toad

(This ditty may be sung to the tune of "A Pub With No Beer")

Ed Gierek was Polish and so was his toad,
for whom he'd composed a magnificent ode.
When Melsor the toad wished to hear a good tune,
the Great Edvard Gierek would commence to croon:

Refrain:
"We'll raise high the wages and keep prices low,
we'll borrow the difference and pay as we go
'Cause the people want trabants to drive out to view
their socialist comrades all lined in a queue."

The heroes of socialist labor all toiled
to assure that the Five Year Plan wouldn't be spoiled,
And the communist leaders who had nothing to gain
would smile to their comrades and intoned this refrain:

Refrain:
"We'll raise high the wages and keep prices low,
we'll borrow the difference and pay as we go
'Cause the people want trabants to drive out to view
their socialist comrades all lined in a queue."

To purchase the foods that they wanted to eat
the comrades would queue up right in the street,
The shops opened at ten but you shouldn't be late,
so get in the queue before half past eight:

Refrain:
"We'll raise high the wages and keep prices low,
we'll borrow the difference and pay as we go,
'Cause the people want toilets to take in the view
of comrades outside lining up in a queue."

Mobuto's pig

Mobuto had a well-dressed pig that he kept on hand
to lend advice on how to rule his complicated land.
The pig was very smart indeed and got just what it wanted
and pranced around in fancy clothes and jewelry which it flaunted.

The pig had lots of plans in mind – all in preparation,
to help the people of Zaire and glorify the nation.
Then one day there were reports that UFOs had landed,
and rumors were soon buzzing 'round about what they'd demanded.

The pig decided it was best to find the crew and greet them,
for when it comes to aliens, it's always best to meet them.
The aliens had come from far and had some fine inventions.
They'd been so long in transit they'd forgotten their intentions.

The aliens were four-feet tall and breathing through their eyes
and when Mobuto saw them – well, let's say he was surprised.
Mobuto was confused at first and sat there looking dumb.
The aliens said nothing clear and just began to hum.

It was the pig who saved the day, suggesting decorations.
Mobuto decked them out with medals and called them sons of nations.
The aliens were offered homes in Zaire's finest districts
but they decided to return taking only biscuits.

The pig will be remembered for many were inspired,
But Mobuto has now left the scene: you could say he's retired.

Enver, don't shoot!

Enver Hoxha – he knew French,
he had the best seat on the bench.
He knew Shehu from the start,
abolished taxes: that was smart,
built some bunkers 'cross the land,
half a million – that was grand.
All the while he thought he knew
that Mehmet Shehu would be true.

Mehmet Shehu was a hoot!
His last words were "Enver don't shoot!"
As he loaded up his gun,
He shouted "There's just one number one."
"Enver, don't shoot! Enver, don't shoot!"
His last words were "Enver, don't shoot!"

Shehu was prime minister,
some said that he was sinister.
He was tough – now that's for sure,
For his foes, death was the cure.
Skanderbeg had a "giant mind"
or so he revealed to humankind.
Mao Zedong inspired him,
but the Little Red Book – it tired him.

Mehmet Shehu was a hoot!
His last words were "Enver don't shoot!"
As he loaded up his gun,

He shouted "There's just one number one."
"Enver, don't shoot! Enver, don't shoot!"
His last words were "Enver, don't shoot!"

Then they quarreled and they split,
Enver Hoxha threw a fit.
And when he needed a problem solver,
he just reached for his revolver.
"Mehmet Shehu, you've betrayed
the party and it's time you paid
for your independent point of view.
Now it's time to say adieu."

Mehmet Shehu was a hoot!
His last words were "Enver don't shoot!"
As he loaded up his gun,
He shouted "There's just one number one."
"Enver, don't shoot! Enver, don't shoot!"
His last words were "Enver, don't shoot!"

Enver Hoxha had decided
Shehu would be "suicided"
Shehu left a little note,
Said it was an accident and I quote,
"I cleaned my gun and took a breath,
and then it went off and caused my death."
Or maybe it was suicide,
plain and simple: you decide.

Mehmet Shehu was a hoot!
His last words were "Enver don't shoot!"
As he loaded up his gun,
He shouted "There's just one number one."
"Enver, don't shoot! Enver, don't shoot!"
His last words were "Enver, don't shoot!"

Saparmurat Niazov Turkmenbashi's orchard of unicorns

Turkmenbashi, man of gold, you rule a land both rich and old,
you know the thoughts in people's minds, you know that love of nation binds
children of this land as one. Who knows what deeds will yet be done?
Here's the truth I will describe: Turkmenbashi leads our tribe.

In your orchard I have seen, unicorns so strong and lean,
I have seen you thinking hard, your own pains you disregard,
while you try to find the way to lead your people from disarray.
I have seen you taking time to write inspired lines in rhyme.

Many streets are named for you, that is right, that is your due.
Our vodka bottles make some space on their labels for your face.
And when a meteor came down, landing near a Turkmen town,
You named it for yourself and stated, that it should be celebrated.

You've written moral guidelines too, which our children must read through.
You banned gold teeth and gold tooth caps, you know that those are dentists' traps.
A palace of ice should be erected, and for its location you selected
The middle of the desert plain – in Karakum, a hot domain.

You renamed all the months and days, you inspired a poetry craze,
with your insights and your wit, such as my very favorite,
"Only a Turkmen can make a Turkmen out of a Turkmen."
You asked your unicorns for advice, on how to build a paradise.

Some people want to criticize, I just want to eulogize
your noble deeds, your one-horned steeds
your posture and your choice of suits.
Count me among your loyal recruits.

(The line "Only a Turkmen can make a Turkmen out of a Turkmen"
is taken from Michael Krakovskiy, "Deadprogrammerbashi", at
Deadprogrammers' Café, at <u>www.deadprogrammer.com/?p=1262</u> [accessed
on 11 August 2007].)

Welcome in Libya

Welcome in Libya, heterosexual men
and attractive women under 35.
Please dress modestly,
remember that the Brother Leader
and King of Culture
loves you
and expects you to love him
in return.
Love means respect:
since you will love the Brother Leader,
you will show respect for him,
not criticize his rule
or his country
or his religion
or his tribe
or his family
or the Libyan media
or the Kufra oasis project.
Remember too:
there is no corruption in Libya,
only rewards for the deserving.
Would anyone deny
that the deserving deserve what they deserve?
Of course not!
Welcome in Libya!

Die gute Zeiten rollen lassen

(Verse written to recall that Otto Grotewohl was chairman of the Council of Ministers from 1949 to 1964 in the East German SED, as the communist party was called, and that local East Germans would raise their glasses of wine, in his time, with a toast, "Zum Wohl, zum Grotewohl!", meaning "To your health, to Grotewohl!", a pun on his name. In an unrelated allusion, the verse recalls that the Vikings reckoned their tax in quantities of butter.)

Hier in Leipzig vi like relax
vi like pretend vi don't pay tax,
vi pull down pants und bare our asses,
den vi raise up high our glasses
und vi shout out loud und clear:
"Ja, vi like it living hier
in our socialistic land
und singing mit de marching band.
Sure, let the good times roll,
die gute Zeiten rollen lassen!"

Tax man makes heads spin und flutter
but vi tell, "Vi pay with butter.
Vi have buckets, vi drive Wagen,
how much butter is you magen?
Vi sind nicht Vikings but vi like
wenn de taxes do not hike.
Ja, vi like it living hier
in our socialistic land
und singing mit de marching band.
Sure, let the good times roll,
die gute Zeiten rollen lassen!"

Come and see our waterfall,
raise your glass and say "Zum Wohl!"
Venn you've drunk a couple glass
then you say "Zum Grotewohl!"

but you know the party's right,
this seems certain venn you're tight,
When you ready now you say
"Ich trink' zur ganzen SED!"
Now we've had some alcohol,
ja zum Wohl und Grotewohl!
Best it's time for lemon frenzy
squeeze the juice into your tea
spoon in honey, stir and sip,
just leave bisschen yet for me.

RELIGION

Were Adam and Eve really married?

God made a human and liked him so much,
he gave him a garden to till,
but Adam played solitaire sunrise to dusk
and his boredom was making him ill.
So he called out to God and he had a request:
he explained that he was all alone.
So God said, "OK, I'll make you a bride;
just give me some flesh and a bone."
And so it was done and a woman named Eve
turned up and said, "Let us not tarry,
but let's call on the Father to join us together.
It only makes sense that we marry."
So God said to them, "You'll be needing a priest,
'cause only a priest is empowered
to join folks like you in marriage so true
before you both end up deflowered."
So God plucked a hair from Eve's crown so fair
and said "Come on, let's get down to business."
And a priest soon appeared, roman collar and beard,
And recited his chant for his listeners:
"We find we are gathered together right here,
To join these two folks in some bliss,
but where are the best man and maiden of honor
and what of the ring – is it missing?
OK, we'll dispense with the usual rites,
and get down to basics and *do* you?
I hear you are yessing, there's no need for guessing,
I declare you both married. We're through."
And marriage is this: two consenting adults

who agree to take care of each other,
with love and respect, and converse unto death,
and see it as joy, not as bother.

The meals of Friar Aquinotle

Refrain:
That noble friar Aquinotle
drank his milk straight from the bottle
and in his quest for certitude
drew inspiration from his food.

At breakfast he thought ham was odd
tho' it recalled the Lamb of God,
a fried tomato rich and red
reminded him how Jesus bled,
three scrambled eggs in the vicinity
inspired thoughts of the Holy Trinity,
and fried potatoes circling round
reminded him how Christ was crowned.

Refrain:
That noble friar Aquinotle
drank his milk straight from the bottle
and in his quest for certitude
drew inspiration from his food.

When Aquinotle sat for lunch
most usually he had a hunch
that as he'd start to eat his meal,
important truths would be revealed.
A slice of piglet on his plate
could help him to elucidate
the joys of heaven, pains of hell,
while waiting for the dinner bell.

Refrain:
That noble friar Aquinotle
drank his milk straight from the bottle
and in his quest for certitude
drew inspiration from his food.

At dinner time – why, that meant broth!
And more analogies for men of the cloth,
and as he ate without restraint
he thought of all of heaven's saints,
upon the Godhead he reflected,
rose from his seat and genuflected,
sorry that he was a sinner
and then returned to finish dinner.

Chorus of the Holy Fathers

The Holy Fathers: Buon Giorno! A good day! Buon Giorno!
The sun is leaping in the sky. My, oh my.
The clouds are oozing across the blue. Wouldn't you?
When I saw the pretty lake, I did a double-take.
They say there's trouble in the air: I don't care.
The birds are high – the fish are deep.
I took a peep, and so I know.
The hills are rolling, the bears are strolling.
And elephants are really heavy.
Buon Giorno! It means "good day"!
And a good day it is for feasting well. I feel swell.

The 10 commandments: you shouldn't bend them.
Indulgences, we recommend them.
If I had an indulgence for every saint in heaven
Then, I swear upon my reliquary,
I'd be pleased as punch just like the day
I finished at the seminary.
I swear upon St. Peter's toe, that I'll protect each embryo,
I swear upon St. Thomas' rib, that I will never doubt or fib,
I swear upon St. Andrew's chin, that I'll maintain my discipline,
I swear upon St. Catherine's brows, that I will honor all my vows,
I swear upon St. Mary's waist, that I'll stay celibate and chaste,
I swear upon St. Gertrude's breasts, that I'll be brave with all life's tests,
I swear upon St. Debbie's ass, that I'll never covet any lass,
And I swear upon St. Jimmy's limbs, that I will always sing my hymns.

We don't need life's distractions, we don't need vain abstractions,
what we need is time for prayer and for robust benefactions.
Buon Giorno! It means "good day!" Buon Giorno!

[They all toast and drink.]

In heaven, the saints eat tomatoes

(In Croatian, the word for heaven is "raj" and the word for tomato is "rajčica." Could there be a connection? This verse explores this important issue.)

In heaven, the saints eat tomatoes,
the angels eat nothing at all,
except for their boxes of chocolates:
with chocolates they have such a ball.

In heaven, the saints eat tomatoes,
they know they are good for the heart,
but growing tomatoes in heaven
entails both some talent and art.

In heaven, the saints eat tomatoes.
God, when he eats, prefers pears.
And when it is meal-time in heaven,
they all sit on benches and chairs.

In heaven, the saints eat tomatoes,
drink juices from fruit on the vine.
All heaven's arranged as a kitchen,
with places to sit and to dine.

In heaven, the saints eat tomatoes,
this news is important for you.
I think it is written down somewhere,
I know it because it is true.

In heaven, the saints eat tomatoes,
that's their reward for all time.
The meaning of life is tomatoes:
so be good, avoid evil and crime.

He earned indulgence, yes!

(Composed to the rhythm of "Drill, ye tarriers, drill", an American song dating from 1888. The original lyrics of "Drill, ye tarriers, drill" have been attributed to Thomas Casey, with Charles Connelly credited with having composed the accompanying music. Dedicated to the memory of Pope Clement VI.)

Every Saturday afternoon
down to the church walked Mr. Moon,
worked the garden so he'd win
indulgence from the stain of sin.
He earned indulgence, yes!
And no need to confess.
For it's work all day and working really hard
in the parish church's yard:
he earned indulgence, yes! That's one stain less.

Mr. Moon then figured out
he's pay a friend to take his route,
to work the garden for the priest:
that had merit at the least.
He earned indulgence, yes!
And no need to confess.
For his money was his calling card,
for work done in the church's yard.
He earned indulgence, yes! That's one stain less.

Then one day at seven o'clock
his buddy quit – that was a shock!
But the pastor said that if he paid
the church directly, that was aid
to buy indulgence, yes!
And no need to confess.
For you pay your way in the chapel by the bay,
waiting for the Judgment Day.
He earned indulgence, yes! That's one stain less.

In the confessional

(For Chris)

Sinner: Bless me, father, for I have sinned,
more transgressions in the wind.
Two weeks now are in the bin,
since my last confession: here are my sins.
I was having a lark, just lying around,
so I fed the lark and went into town.
I needed some cash, so I went to the bank,
for the queue so long, whom should I thank?
But I wasn't prepared to wait too long,
so I raised my voice, shouting "Honga pong-pong!"
I brandished my lark and a fish that stank,
and with that succeeded in robbing the bank.
As I finished, I spied a cop by the door,
so I kicked him in the shins and he dropped to the floor.
Bless me, father, that is all I can remember.

Priest: Well, my son, surely you have tweaked
the truth a little, since in just two weeks,
it is hard to believe you'd slip into sin,
robbing a bank – what made you begin?
And just two weeks, are you quite sure
that you were just here for a salvific cure?

Sinner: Yes, reverend father, I am quite certain,
I remember your confessional and your dark cotton curtain.
But I'm a nice fellow, not nasty or mean,
so give me absolution and wipe my slate clean.

Priest: Well, OK, but your tale is very scary –
for your absolution you should say a "Hail Mary".

Two hours later
Sinner: Bless me father, I'm a winner,
but every now and then, a sinner.
I did the penance you exacted
but soon after got distracted.
It has been two hours since my last confession, here with you,
and these are my sins.

Priest: Well, almighty God is gracious
and his heart is truly spacious.
But I'm not God and I can't see
why you're sinning so merrily.
Just two hours and now you're back!
You're probably a kleptomaniac!

Sinner: Not this time, most reverend father,
and believe me please that I would rather
sun myself on sandy beaches
or scratch my skin to pull out leaches,
than have to ask for absolution
yet again and in rhymed locution.
But as I left your celestial building,
I spied your altar with its golden gilding.
So I rolled it down the aisle, cluck-cluck,
and loaded it onto my pick-up truck.
Then I headed to the police station
in a state of most extreme elation.
I've always liked the front desk there
and the police chief's swivel chair.
So I rolled them out the station's door:
the police don't have them any more.
These were heavy but, cluck-cluck,
I loaded them onto my pick-up truck.
I'll sell this furniture some day
and post these items on ebay.

Bless me, though I may have omitted
other sins which I committed
in the two hours I've been gone –
so absolve me please and let's move on.

Priest: Well, stealing from the Church, your mother,
rather than from some other –
this is serious and it's quite perverse
and, yes, it's even somewhat worse
than robbing banks and kicking shins:
these are, in fact, substantial sins.
But three "Hail Marys" might suffice,
provided you promise to be nice
and your sinning to decrease.
You are forgiven: go in peace.
...

By the way, let me know when you post my altar on ebay.

O mamma, are you a virgin?

(This may be sung as blues song.)

I get up mornings and ask myself,
Who's my father? – that great elf,
in the sky or some other,
who had sex with you, dear mother?
O mamma, are you a virgin?
Hey mamma, are you a virgin?

It happened once, I know for certain,
a virgin birth – up went the curtain!
And if a first time, why not twice?
What are the odds? – just roll the dice!
O mamma, I'm eatin' sturgeon,
O mamma, are you a virgin?

Is my father really Dad?
I have a theory that makes me glad:
it just could be I'm the Son of God –
don't look at me as if I'm odd!
O mamma, God is a surgeon,
Hey mamma, are you a virgin?

PHILOSOPHICAL RUMINATIONS

Tea with Aunt Mabel

Aunt Mabel called, invited us
to join her for a spot of tea,
but on her kitchen table top
was something you don't often see:
a hologram of Nietzsche's teeth,
clearly marked, so no mistake,
but room enough on every side
for cups of tea and lots of cake.
We asked Aunt Mabel what's it for.
She said, "Just decoration."
"But Nietzsche's teeth?" we were surprised.
Said she, "It's no abomination."
She was quite right, I'll grant you that,
and whose teeth would be finer
than those of such a major man,
a thinker – no one minor.
We looked around her lovely house,
and peeked inside the shower;
what did we find? I think you've guessed:
a bust of Schopenhauer.
And out on the veranda,
perched up next to the stucco,
she had placed a life-size statue
of the Frenchman Michel Foucault.
But what the most surprised me –
there I saw him on her roof,
poised like Santa by her chimney,
but it was François Noel Babeuf.
Aunt Mabel likes philosophers,
she also likes her tea;
I'm just glad her crazy genes
have no part in me.

Machiavelli on the streets of Firenze

(May be sung to the tune of "The Streets of Laredo," a traditional song popularized by Johnny Cash and Arlo Guthrie, among others)

When Machiavelli grew up in Firenze
the land was in turmoil and torn up by war,
rampaging soldiers swept down and sacked Roma.
The Italian people could take it no more.

In Firenze, his city, the Medicis held power
until they were thrown out by a large angry mob,
For Machiavelli this would prove auspicious
The republic soon hired him and gave him a job.

For the next 18 years he would work for his city,
It was a republic – which is what he liked best.
But then the Medicis came back into power,
They snuffed the republic with vengeance and zest.

So Machiavelli was packed off to prison
but he pleaded 'not guilty' and soon was released,
He wanted to find a way back into service
but the man who could help him soon was deceased.

He wrote *The Discourses* and drafted *The Prince,*
He considered that violence was useful at times,
And when politicians kill critics and rivals,
these actions are justified, they are not crimes.

Winning is wonderful, losing is lousy –
So said Machiavelli, who lost in the end.
The Medicis contracted a book from the author
But when they collapsed, he was left without friends.

As I was a-walking the streets of Firenze
I spied Machiavelli or, rather, his ghost.
I asked him what mattered, he said it was power,
Power that mattered to him uppermost.

But Machiavelli is long dead and buried,
In a church in Firenze he rests in his tomb,
But just you imagine him soaring above us,
eating a coconut chick chicka-boom!

Spinoza

(May be sung to the tune of "Nel blu dipinto di blu (Volare)", 1958, music & original lyrics by Domenico Modugno and Franco Migliacci)

When I remember to tell you I'll tell you a tale,
maybe you've heard it but it's one that never grows stale.
It's of a fabulous thinker who thought very hard,
and his conclusions may catch you sometimes off guard.

Spinoza, hah hah
Spinoza, wo-wo-wo-wo
He wanted the people to read
what he wrote and he knew they would need
some good glasses with focus
and no hocus-pocus
and so he would grind them a lens,
but he breathed in the dust
and died prematurely and bust.

Quite surely, yeah yeah
Spinoza wo-wo-wo-wo
His clothing was all made of satin,
he wrote all his works out in Latin:
Yes, his *Ethics, Tractatus*
and one more *Tractatus,*
this thinker was writing a ton,
but the clergy inspected
his book and rejected that one.

Spinoza yeah yeah
Spinoza wo-wo-wo-wo
He wanted the people to heed
his notions and therefore to read,
he wanted the people to heed
his notions and therefore to read…
(böp böp)

Taxidermy daddy (Jeremy Bentham)

(a hootenanny)

Taxidermy daddy, you're always on my mind:
All I want is the greatest good for all of humankind.

When you were young or sort of young
you had a friend called James,
who had a clever son called John
who liked to play with games.
But you and James decided that
young John could do much more
than sit around and play and shout
and eat and sleep and snore.

Taxidermy daddy, you're always on my mind:
All I want is the greatest good for all of humankind.

You planned his education
and you rearranged his life,
You even thought you'd try your hand
at picking him a wife.
You planned a massive program
and tutored John Stuart Mill,
but then he had a breakdown
and he started to feel ill.

Taxidermy daddy, you're always on my mind:
All I want is the greatest good for all of humankind.

You had a scheme for prison life
to make surveillance work:

panopticons were on your mind,
you drove your friends beserk.
You never missed a meeting
at your college and you said,
"I wouldn't want to miss one –
not even when I'm dead."
So when you went to heaven,
you had your body stuffed,
'cause of meetings of the faculty
you never had enough.

Taxidermy daddy, you're always on my mind:
All I want is the greatest good for all of humankind.

Dancing Mind-to-Mind
(Georg Wilhelm Friedrich Hegel)

(May be sung to the tune of Irving Berlin's "Cheek to cheek," 1935)

Hegel, I love Hegel
especially when I think I'm so inclined
And I must have sought the happiness I find
When I read 'Phenomenology of Mind'.

Oh the rational has reason
and there's ethics in the state
and you're free when you obey the law,
'cause that's the human fate.

Oh the Absolute is given
in whatever is around:
And there're duties everywhere you look:
at least that's what he found.

Absolute!
I want to contemplate truth,
to cogitate Truth,
it helps to make sense of…

Hegel, I love Hegel,
especially when I think I'm so inclined,
And I must have sought the happiness I find
when I read 'Phenomenology of Mind'.

Salvation through Hegel

Georg Wilhelm Friedrich Hegel –
read his books, get in the loop,
pay our fee and read our fliers,
be a member of our group.

Georg Wilhelm Friedrich Hegel –
that's a name you hear a lot:
that's because of all his insights
and the concepts that he's got.

Georg Wilhelm Friedrich Hegel –
so profound and never trite.
Come and listen to the lectures,
held on every Wednesday night.

Georg Wilhelm Friedrich Hegel:
there, I've said it once again.
If you hear his words each Wednesday,
you'll get answers for life's pain.

Georg Wilhelm Friedrich Hegel –
it's the state you must obey.
Your knowledge can be Absolute,
join our group without delay!

That's Bakunin

(May be sung to the tune of "That's amore" [Harry Warren])

When the bomb hits the air
like a hydrogen flare,
that's Bakunin! That's Bakunin!
When the talk of the town
is to bring the state down –
that's Bakunin! That's Bakunin!

Can you bring a match? Can you light the fuse?
Can you give a speech? Can you try to use
elocution? elocution?
'Cause we want to rouse everyone awake
so that we can plan how we're gonna make
revolution, revolution…

When the bomb hits the air
like a hydrogen flare –
that's Bakunin! That's Bakunin!
When the talk of the town
is to bring the state down
that's Bakunin! That's Bakunin!

Wie einst, Platon-Liebling

(May be sung to the tune of "Lili Marlene" [1938], music by Norbert Schultze)

When I'm reading Plato, I can see the truth
All the politicians – they seem so uncouth,
They're living in an ill-lit cave,
they don't know how they should behave,
but Plato, he's my guide
but Plato, he's my guide.

Tom Aquinas wanted people to be good
so that we would do exactly what we should,
He wrote about the Natural Law
'cause knowing what he knew he saw,
Morality seemed given
Morality seemed clear.

Hegel helps us realize, if we are confused,
the problem may be that our brains are barely used.
If every cow looks black to you
it may be darkest night to you,
But Hegel brings the sun out,
but Hegel brings the sun.

Finally, I'm thinking, on this I will insist:
René Descartes once told us, we think and thus exist.
If we did not exist in time,
we would not think or speak in rhyme.
Thus, those who've not existed,
have neither thought nor sung,
yes, those who've not existed,
have neither thought nor sung.

In Friedrich Nietzsche's brain

(May be sung to the theme of the television program "The Addams Family", which aired from 1964 to 1966; the musical theme was composed by Vic Mizzy)

The Übermensch is rising
and what he sees he's prizing,
the whole world is cap-sizing
in Friedrich Nietzsche's brain.

"God is dead," he shouted –
of that he never doubted,
or dogmas they were flouted
in Friedrich Nietzsche's brain.

....plain
....pain
....insane.

So read him, if you're thinking
your own ideas are stinking.
You will enjoy your swinking
in Friedrich Nietzsche's brain.

AMERICANA

A message from the Minnesota tourist bureau

In almost every place we've been,
that we recall, at least,
the sunset's always in the west
and sunrise in the east.
But it's the other way around
on Minnesota's farms,
where crimson sunsets in the west
can stir some real alarm.

In other states, we've heard it told,
it is the dogs that bark,
while cats will purr and sometimes meow
and cling onto the bark.
But here in Minneapolis
it is the dogs that meow
and cats that chase the postman
and bark and say bow-wow.

In other lands and cities,
you sit down on your chair,
but here in Minnesota
you're floating in the air.
At breakfast, lunch and dinner
the food is floating by,
it's lighter than the air you breathe
and you are flying high.

So visit Minnesota
enjoy our special shade.
You won't be disappointed,
no need to be afraid.
So just come on 'round and visit us!

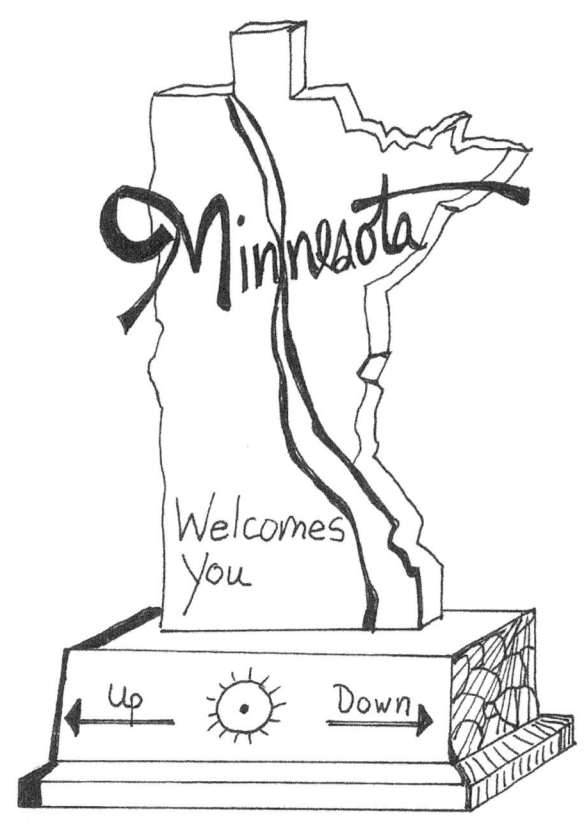

Seventeen cowboys

(Inspired by the melody of Stephen Collins Foster's "Beautiful Dreamer," and with not-so-subtle allusions to Karl Marx's "German Ideology")

Seventeen cowboys up on a hill,
packin' some whiskey, takin' a swill,
brandin' some cattle, yodeling too,
if you could join them, now wouldn't you?

Finding a clearing, soon they will stop,
build a few cabins, settin' up shop,
fetchin' a guí-tar, strummin' some chords,
livin' like this and no one gets bored.

Hunt in the mornin', then you go fish,
rear cattle near evenin', food on the dish,
then you can criticize, after your meal,
say what you're thinkin', whatever you feel.

The problem is money – there just ain't enough,
them folks that got it, treatin' us rough.
Time is a-comin' when cowboys will ride,
and lasso the bossman, tannin' his hide.

William Walker, King of Nicaragua

A lad was born on the 8th of May
In eighteen hundred twenty four
His parents shouted "hip hooray!"
And tap-danced on the timber floor.
Young William Walker had some brains
And finished college at fourteen,
He went 'round Europe, riding trains,
All the while he was assorting
Ideas that he'd put to use
In the conquests that he planned
To see English more diffuse
-- it was the tongue at his command.

Refrain:
> *English should be the language of choice*
> *When Nicaraguans want to give voice*
> *To their opinions and to their conceptions.*
> *English should be the language of choice.*

He started with medicine, thinking he would
hang out his shingle as a fresh MD,
Then he changed his mind and took up law,
But soon came down with some bad ennui.
So he gathered rangers who swore they would
Practice conquests where they could.
In Mexico they began their trade,
Declared a republic and built a stockade.

<u>Expanded refrain</u>:
> *English should be the language of choice*
> *When Nicaraguans want to give voice*
> *To their opinions and to their conceptions.*
> *English should be the language of choice.*
>
> *Why speak in Spanish when you can choose*
> *American English, which you can use*
> *When you're in Boston or out in India?*
> *English should be the language you use.*

He talked with his men and they were sure
that Nicaraguans would be glad
to see them coming so demure;
they would know that Walker had
the means to end their slavery
and praise his virile bravery.

<u>Re-expanded refrain</u>:
> *English should be the language of choice*
> *When Nicaraguans want to give voice*
> *To their opinions and to their conceptions.*
> *English should be the language of choice.*
>
> *Why speak in Spanish when you can choose*
> *American English, which you can use*
> *When you're in Boston or out in India?*
> *English should be the language you use.*
>
> *If you speak English, everyone knows*
> *The point of the sentences that you compose.*
> *Why be content to be not understood,*
> *When you have English, which everyone knows.*

Walker and company marched and marched,
Their stomachs ached, their mouths were parched.
But they beat the army, won their goal,
And in the country took control.

Further expanded refrain:
> *English should be the language of choice*
> *When Nicaraguans want to give voice*
> *To their opinions and to their conceptions.*
> *English should be the language of choice.*

> *Why speak in Spanish when you can choose*
> *American English, which you can use*
> *When you're in Boston or out in India?*
> *English should be the language you use.*
> *If you speak English, everyone knows*
> *The point of the sentences that you compose.*
> *Why be content to be not understood,*
> *When you have English, which everyone knows.*

> *Time to be strong, not to be weak,*
> *So pass a law to make everyone speak*
> *The language you like 'cause you know that it is,*
> *Time to be strong, not to be weak.*

Walker established himself as a king
Of fair Nicaragua – that was the thing.
For three years he reigned and everyone cheered
For this clean-shaven man with no moustache or beard!
But then the Hondurans captured this guy,
They pummeled his bottom and they made him cry,
They brought out the rifles while he held his breath,
That was the day that he met his death.

Final refrain:
> *English should be the language of choice*
> *When Nicaraguans want to give voice*
> *To their opinions and to their conceptions.*
> *English should be the language of choice.*

Warren G. Harding's teapot

Warren G. Harding liked to drink tea
Teapot and biscuits by the sea
But he didn't like to drink alone
So he built himself a Teapot Dome.
Warren – you please me so,
And you let the good times flow.

One lump or two lumps, as you please,
Add a little scandal and a lot of sleaze,
If you've got a government
Corruption is its fundament.
Warren – I like your hair,
And you look so debonair.

An honest politician's like a rose
Without a scent, I do suppose:
Find a politician who's a little bent –
He's like a rose that has some scent!
Warren – you're number one
In the galaxy of fun.

Warren hated being president
Or in the White House resident:
Too many duties, too much work –
It's enough to drive a man beserk.
Warren – you please me so,
And you let the good times flow.

But he did not fill his term,
Died in office – the facts are firm.
Then Calvin Coolidge took his place
And did his best to keep the pace.
But Warren – you're number one
In the galaxy of fun.

His speeches were renowned for length,
Though maybe grammar was not his strength.
But when I go to bed at night,
I think of Warren, who was always right.
Warren – you're number one
In the galaxy of fun.

J. Edgar Hoover's coming to town

(May be sung to the tune of "Santa Claus is coming to town")

You better not rat, you better not spy
You best not defect, I'm telling you why
J. Edgar Hoover's coming to town!
You better not rat, you better not spy
You best not defect, I'm telling you why
J. Edgar Hoover's coming to town!

He knows if you're a commie
He knows if you're a red
He knows if you are hiding
Lenin's works under your bed.

So you better watch out,
You better not spy
'cause he's got the clout
To make you cry.
J. Edgar Hoover's coming to town!
He's making a list and checking it twice,
He already knows who's naughty and nice.
J. Edgar Hoover's coming to town!

He might be in a frilly dress
He might have makeup on
But he will always catch his man,
'cause the guy is plenty strong.

You better not rat, you better not spy
You best not defect, I'm telling you why
J. Edgar Hoover's coming to town!

He's making a list and checking it twice,
He already knows who's naughty and nice.
J. Edgar Hoover's coming to town!
J. Edgar Hoover's coming to town!
J. Edgar Hoover's coming to town!

If the mayor were a pigeon

If the mayor were a pigeon, there is much that he could do
like make some wise decisions about the public loo.
Why build a lot of toilets, thus fostering enslavement
to sitting on the toilet seat when there's space right on the pavement?
If people would just realise, as pigeons surely do,
how vastly more convenient and more efficient too,
it is to simply find relief the moment that you feel
the slightest urge in that regard, they'd ape the birds with zeal.
And think about the meals we eat, with plates and forks and knives,
and all the soap and water used to wash them through our lives.
But pigeons -- glad you asked me -- dine right on the street,
they don't use knives or forks or plates and yet they keep quite neat.
They never wash the dishes or purchase cups or plates,
they never go on diets, 'cause they never watch their weights.
They use the public fountain to give themselves a bath,
the water's fine, come jump right in -- hey, you can do the math.
You'll never have to clean the tub or stock your shelf with soap.
So when election time arrives, the pigeon wants your vote.

At the polls

(For Torbjørn, who inspired this verse)

When I go to cast my vote, I want a dude what don't smell bad,
who's got no roaches in his hair, and one who's not entirely mad.
Important that his socks must match, his shirt should not be inside out.
I like it too that when he speaks he doesn't rave or scream or shout.
I don't much care if he can think or what his politics might be,
as long as how he's gonna vote won't bring harm to you or me.
I want a dude who walks to work or maybe sometimes takes the bus,
a guy what's got a Maine Coon cat, about which pet he makes a fuss.
I'm gonna like it if he whistles, nice and low like a bassoon,
and even if it's just one note, I'm sure I'll hear a lovely tune.
But most important is this fact: he oughta wear a cowboy hat
and strut around in cowboy boots, inhabiting his habitat.

Stopgap, Kansas

More than a truck stop, less than a town,
Stopgap, Kansas, got it all
got a wayside chapel and a fillin' pump
got a general store at the shoppin' mall
got a bowlin' alley and cinema flicks,
at the handyman store you can buy your bricks.

On Saturday evening you can mosey on down,
put on your skates and skate aroun'.
More than a truck stop, less than a town,
Stopgap, Kansas got it all –
If you think I'm kiddin', jess take a look,
here in Stopgap have a ball!

THE ANIMAL WORLD

Possible rabbits in this house

There are no rabbits in this house.
But ask a philosopher,
how many possible rabbits are there
in this house?
None, you say?
But we do not speak of real rabbits,
only of possible ones
or do you believe for a moment
that no rabbits are possible in this house?
No, you cannot say that!
There are no rabbits in this house,
but rabbits are possible.
So we ask again,
how many possible rabbits are in this house?
Sixty-three, you say?
Why not sixty-four?
Four hundred?
Why not four hundred and one?
An infinite number, you say?
Don't be silly – that is meaningless.
The correct answer is:
the number of possible rabbits in this house
cannot be determined.
Now you know.

All aboard, kitties!

*(This rhyme mimics the sound of an old-fashioned train.
For Morten Kulen)*

The kitties decide
shorf shorf
to go for a ride
shorf shorf
they're packin' their bags
shorf shorf
and wavin' their flags
shorf shorf
ya wanna go far?
shorf shorf
a train or a car
shorf shorf
will prove to be best
shorf shorf
the kitties go west
shorf shorf
at quarter to two
shorf shorf
they line in the queue
shorf shorf
and get on the train
shorf shorf
it's startin' to rain
shorf shorf
but kitties have seats
shorf shorf
and plenty of treats
shorf shorf

like tuna and seal
shorf shorf
it's time for a meal
shorf shorf
they take in the view
shorf shorf
well, how do you do?
shorf shorf

Lions and tigers

Lions and tigers sleep all day
They don't have to work for pay
They just lie around and snore
Then they turn and sleep some more.

Horses and donkeys like the ground,
Since they want to trot around
They're not going any-where,
They're just happy being there.

Otters and beavers like to swim
That's the way they stay so trim,
They will also dam up streams
Working in their day-shift teams.

Bunnies and weasels are big friends,
They share lettuce and carrot ends,
They can dance and they can sing,
They can do most anything.

Who let the ants come in?

(Sing to the tune of "The E-R-I-E canal," a song written sometime in the 1800s by an unknown songster)

Oh, the ants smell something rotten,
their body odor's bad,
they also need some mouthwash but
they treat it like a fad.

(Hey) we had a swig of whiskey
and we had a round of gin,
but looking 'round we ask ourselves,
who let the ants come in?
who let the ants come in?

The chocolate donuts sprouted wings,
they're flying all around,
and sometimes donut crumbs fall down
to ants down on the ground.

(Hey) we had a swig of whiskey
and we had a round of gin,
but looking 'round we ask ourselves,
who let the ants come in?
who let the ants come in?

We see the lights go flicker,
the moon came in the door,
but looking down we see the ants
are marching 'cross the floor.

(Hey) we had a swig of whiskey
and we had a round of gin,
but looking 'round we ask ourselves,
who let the ants come in?
who let the ants come in?

The walls have started talking,
they say they want to dance,
but most of all they want to talk
about the local ants.

(Hey) we had a swig of whiskey
and we had a round of gin,
but looking 'round we ask ourselves,
who let the ants come in?
who let the ants come in?

The ants have got it very rough,
at least from what I've seen:
four hundred males per colony
for just a single queen.

(Hey) we had a swig of whiskey
and we had a round of gin,
but looking 'round we ask ourselves,
who let the ants come in?
who let the ants come in?

So far it's humans who have ruled
-- and you've seen what that's worth,
but maybe it's the time to make
ants masters of the earth,
and looking 'round we ask ourselves,
who let the ants come in,
who let the ants come in?

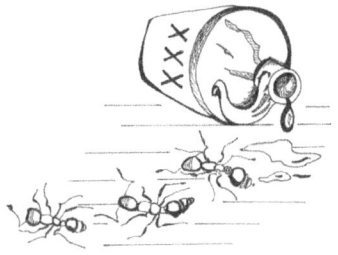

Do crocodiles have ghosts?

Now crocodiles – it is well known – always swim upstream,
this is because – I do suppose – all crocodiles do dream
of living high above the world, upon the mountain tops,
they never do descend and yet the process never stops.

And when these crocodiles expire and draw their final breath,
there is no afterlife for them – no, nothing after death.
So if you think you've seen their ghosts hovering aloof,
then be so kind and furnish me with overwhelming proof.

No, crocodiles are mortal – my friend, he says so too,
and he has seen a lot of them around the city zoo,
and if you've never seen a ghost of some dead crocodile
or seen him part his jaws to spread a Liberace smile,

then that is quite sufficient their existence to deny
'cause these are facts upon the strength of which you can rely.
And so it is I raise my glass to signify a toast
to every deceased crocodiles's nonexistent ghost!

The mystery of feline reproduction

All cats are female,
all dogs are male,
snails have no gender,
snakes are all tail.
Dogs like their kitties,
and here comes a litter –
small hybrid puppies:
they couldn't look fitter.
In a town without dogs
you'll never find kittens:
that's just a matter of history.
Now that you understand
how this is done,
there is no longer a mystery.

LITERATURE, LANGUAGE, REGGAE

Ba-ba-daah

Down in Jamaica in Kingston town
coconut shells grow thick and brown
If you drink lots of coconut milk
your whole body gonna feel like silk
Ba-ba-daah, ba-ba-daah
Ba-ba-daah, ba-ba-daah

Then in the evening you feel like a twirl
Call to the matron and she send you a girl,
You can dance and sing 'til the sky grow pale
'n' *you're* gonna tell a pretty tale
Ba-ba-daah, ba-ba-daah
Ba-ba-daah, ba-ba-daah

If you wanna be King of the bush,
shake your shoulders and swing your tush,
just don't forget that I tell you that
you better off stayin' home on the mat
Ba-ba-daah, ba-ba-daah
Ba-ba-daah, ba-ba-daah
Ba-ba-daah, ba-ba-daah
Ba-ba-daah, ba-ba-daah…

Reggae archaeologicae

I dig all night, I dig all day
I dig through dirt, I dig through clay
What do I find? I find more dirt
Hey you there! I'm no per-vért!
I just like digging 'cause once I found
something exciting stuck in the ground.
I picked it up, what did I see?
Why it was some kinda big brass key –
Now where there's a key, there must be a door
for me what does fate now hold in store?
I looked many years, looked everywhere,
but found no door lying anywhere,
So I gave up the search but not the dig,
and then I found a thingamajig!
It wasn't a door but a piece of vase,
or maybe a chip of a statue's face,
or maybe the edge of a blackbird's wing,
but whatever it was, it made me sing!
Sometimes the years roll by in tens,
with finding nothing – work's intense,
But I tell myself, "you don't despair,
though I chew my nails and bite my hair."
And then success and worldwide fame,
everyone gonna know my name,
'cause I'm the one who found this thing,
to which I've tied a little string.
I know I'm handsome and you wanna flirt,
but all I wanna do is dig in the dirt.
I dig a hole and climb below:

I'm an archaeolo-gíst you know,
I'm living every childhood dream,
this is glory raised supreme.

Oh, Shakespeare was a poet

(This verse may be sung to the tune of "Stewball", a song written by John Herald, Bob Yellen, and Ralph Rinzler, and sung by the popular folk group, Peter, Paul and Mary, beginning in the 1960s)

Oh, Shakespeare was a poet (ba-da ba-da, ba-da ba-da)
and he wrote lots of plays (ba-da ba-da, ba-da ba-da)
He worked in the theater (ba-da ba-da, ba-da ba-da)
to the end of his days (ba-da ba-da, ba-da ba-da).

He wrote a play "Hamlet" (ba-da ba-da, ba-da ba-da),
it dealt with a prince (ba-da ba-da, ba-da ba-da),
whose father was murdered (ba-da ba-da, ba-da ba-da):
it made Hamlet wince (ba-da ba-da, ba-da ba-da).

"The Merchant of Venice" (ba-da ba-da, ba-da ba-da)
was also his work (ba-da ba-da, ba-da ba-da),
The case of poor Portia (ba-da ba-da, ba-da ba-da) –
it drives me berserk (ba-da ba-da, ba-da ba-da).

"Macbeth" is another (ba-da ba-da, ba-da ba-da),
it has lots of blood (ba-da ba-da, ba-da ba-da),
the play has a murder (ba-da ba-da, ba-da ba-da)
and ends with a thud (ba-da ba-da, ba-da ba-da).

He also wrote "Falstaff" (ba-da ba-da, ba-da ba-da)
'bout a corpulent knight (ba-da ba-da, ba-da ba-da)
and Verdi wrote music (ba-da ba-da, ba-da ba-da)
that still can excite (ba-da ba-da, ba-da ba-da).

He wrote more than twenty (ba-da ba-da, ba-da ba-da),
including "King Lear" (ba-da ba-da, ba-da ba-da),
His plays still entrance us (ba-da ba-da, ba-da ba-da),
yes, year after year (ba-da ba-da, ba-da ba-da).

Hey, Shakespeare was a poet (ba-da ba-da, ba-da ba-da)
and he wrote lots of plays (ba-da ba-da, ba-da ba-da)
He worked in the theater (ba-da ba-da, ba-da ba-da)
to the end of his days (ba-da ba-da, ba-da ba-da).

Tribute to Edgar Allan Poe – may he forgive me

(Composed on 29 November 2010; the meter is borrowed from Poe's immortal verse, "Annabel Lee," the last complete poem written by Poe [1849])

It was many and many a poem ago
in Massachusetts state
that a lad was born to a mother soon dead
and grew up in difficult straits
and this lad he enlisted in no other force
than the army – such was his fate.

He decided to take up his pen and write
and earn his pay from verse,
his poems "The Raven" and "Evening Star"
put dollars and cents in his purse.
And he learned the lesson exceedingly well
to never but never be terse.

He married his cousin at twenty-six
but she was half his age,
he published some tales grotesque and strange,
the macabre on every page.
And his readers were thrilled but trembled still:
from this he would earn his wage.

The tales that he wrote tormented some,
this Edgar Allan Poe,
provoking his readers to worry about
all forms of grief and woe:
being buried alive or back from the dead
or facing a zombie foe.

The poet was barely forty when
his health took a turn for dire,
he wandered around on Baltimore's streets
dressed in another's attire,
and then succumbing to heart disease
this talented man expired.

Today we still read his poems and tales,
we shudder and leave on the light,
the darkness scares us terribly much,
since phantoms stalk at night.
But Poe understood the desperate thrill
that comes from vicarious fright.

I speak Splat

Splat's a language very fine,
sounds as sweet as cherry wine,
Yo splat splat means, I speak splat.
Splat ta splat means, Look at that.
Splat means yes, and splat means no.
Splat-splat-splat means, I don't know.
Splat ga splat means, what's the time?
Splat pa splat means, half past nine.
Splat doh splat means, how's it going?
Splat jer splat means, I work for Boeing.
But don't say splatter-splat-splat-splat,
there's no curse as bad as that.

Great Classics summarized in verse

(Inspired by Monty Python's sketch about summarizing Proust in 15 seconds)

In "The Iliad" Agamemnon of Greece was dismayed
because his wife Helen'd been took in a raid.
The Trojans had absconded with her down to Troy
and now he was fuming and angry — oh boy!
So he gathered some soldiers inside a wood horse
and made it look pretty with a ribbon, of course.
The Trojans allowed it inside as a gift,
but when the Greeks jumped out, the Trojans were miffed.

Hermann Melville liked whaling and wanted to write
about how a captain got into a fight
with a whale so enormous it made a huge splash
whenever it leapt through the air with a crash.
Captain Ahab just wanted to catch Moby Dick,
his obsession was gradually making him sick.
So he took his whole crew on a hunt for this whale,
but most of them died — what an unhappy tale!

In "A Tale of Two Cities" Charles Dickens described
some finer impressions that he had imbibed
of troubled revolt in France on the streets
and tried to dispel some misguided conceits.
There were people in England who didn't know French,
their squalid abodes were covered with stench.
There were Frenchmen as well whose English was poor,
some of them living deep down in the sewer.

Dostoyevsky was brilliant, but just a bit shady,
he wrote 'bout a man who killed an old lady.
He'd wanted to prove that he wouldn't conform
to society's pressures and morals and norms.
But old man Porfiry, an inspector and cop,
was intent that he'd manage to put to a stop
Raskolnikov's notions 'bout reaching the stars,
and lock him up firmly, in jail, behind bars.

Christopher Marlowe and his work

Chaucer didn't write his books – he's just some sort of faker –
No, old Chris Marlowe he did that, right after he wrote Shakespeare.
Marlowe wrote the *Scarlet Letter,* also *Moby Dick,*
but other fellows take the credit: boy, it makes me sick.
That Gatsby book – that's Marlowe's work, and likewise *War and Peace.*
And *Don Quixote,* need you ask? Marlowe wrote it while in Nice.
But Marlowe was so occupied with writing other people's books,
he had no time to write his own,
though we too long mistook *Doc Faustus* for the work of Marlowe,
but it wasn't so.
For Shakespeare wrote that book of his, though that was long ago.
So now you have some sense of what you can learn in college,
and this is what we like to call truly special knowledge.

A girl named Lapuca

There once was a girl named Lapuca,
who liked Bach's Toccata and Fuca,
which she played on the flute
with a toodle-dee-toot:
you'd like it, just come take a looka.

There once was a fellow named Biktor,
whose pet was a boa constrictor.
His snake lived on maco,
and smoked some tobacco,
and was a convincing evictor.

There once was a pectopah rated
the best in the gopod and slated
to host inostransi
in skirts or in pantsi,
who wanted to dine and be feted.

There once was a postman named Bopic
who never gave up to be hopik
that one day he'd team
with the girl of his dream,
and together they'd then dance the gopak.

On Dumpledy-Down

On Dumpledy-Down near the church in the vale,
chipmunks and squirrels with big bushy tales,
gather and blather of all sorts of things,
like Shepherdly-Shemp and the songs that he sings.

This Saturday morn', from out of the woods,
come foxes all donning their red riding hoods.
They're looking so proper, just waving their fans,
but where are they going and what are their plans?

It's Shepherdly-Shemp that they're wanting to see:
on that all the foxes entirely agree.
They're eager to hear him trilling his notes,
and want his advice on subjects remote.

On Landerly-Lane they hear serenading:
it's Shepherdly-Shemp and his tune is cascading,
downward and upward, it's easy to hear
why it's his singing brings everyone cheer.

But curious foxes need also advice:
would it be useful and would it be nice
if they would offer a counseling service?
Shemp thinks that's great, no one should be nervous.

So, on Dumpledy-Down they're setting up shop,
giving advice to all who will stop.
What should I wear? What should I do?
Just ask the foxes: they'll give you a clue.

Alice in Limerickland

(Inspired by Lewis Carroll's "Alice in Wonderland" or, more precisely, by seeing three minutes of a ballet on the theme of Carroll's "Alice in Wonderland" on Norwegian television on 24 December)

There once was a maiden named Alice,
who lived in a great crystal palace.
She fell down a hole
that was made by a mole,
or maybe a rabbit, so callous.

A rabbit so white made of plastic
had limbs that were strong and elastic,
while she followed its tail,
it ran up the trail,
into a great hall dynastic.

A green caterpillar was there,
and advised Alice she should beware
of mushrooms around
that grew on the ground:
if she ate them she'd have quite a scare.

Then she encountered a fungus,
she ate it and grew quite humungus.
But that was not all,
since she also shrank small.
The fungus was called omphalotus.

A tea party with a mad hatter
was occasion for laughter and chatter –
"Would you like some more tea?"
"Why that cannot be,
because I've had none, for that matter."

The March Hare just stood for a while,
then replied with a curious smile,
"More than nothing is more,
so don't be a bore,
just accept some more tea without bile."

'Twas tea that she drank from a cup,
was invited to join them for sup
by the hatter and hare,
a jolly gay pair,
just living alone with their pup.

The garden whose roses were painted
had paint fumes and Alice near fainted.
All roses are red,
all violets are blue.
These painters were sorely demainted.

"Why do you paint the flow'rs red,
when a rose can be yellow instead?"
The painters replied
that they merely complied
with commands at the price of their heads.

"Well, none of this makes any sense,
no matter your fine recompense,"
thought Alice aloud,
but the painters were cowed
and continued their work looking tense.

With that Alice let out a laugh
and wandered on down a steep path,
'til she got to a bay
where a game was in play,
with Her Highness, the old psychopath.

The Queen was already at play
at a vigorous game of croquet,

but the rules of the game
were never the same,
when the Queen was the host of the day.

For a mallet she used a flamingo
and grabbed the poor bird by its dingo,
then swung at the ball,
shouting "Death to you all!"
but what did that mean in her lingo?

Alice, of course, had to query,
"How is it Your Highness is merry,
while condemning to death
in a frivolous breath
all present, who find you quite scary?"

But Highness was clearly insane,
especially, you see, in her brain,
ignored what was asked,
and instead she basked
in her glory and spoke this refrain:

"When sheep are fluorescent they glow
on the mountain tops up by the snow;
thanks to jelly fish genes
they glow pink and green –
just ask me how I can know?"

But Alice thought this was absurd,
did not believe even one word,
since the Queen was insane
right in her brain,
and soon forgot what she had heard.

Just then a large cat appeared,
and all round the sans culottes cheered,
since this Cheshire cat knew
everything through and through,
and had beautiful whiskers and beard.

"The truth is much truer than fiction,"
said the cat with most elegant diction.
"So say what you mean,
come on and come clean,
and say it with honest conviction."

"OK," said Alice undaunted
and explained to the cat that she wanted
to just understand
the rules of this land
and not to be mocked or be taunted.

"Well, censorship – that's what that is,"
said the cat and, continuing, "Ms.,
you don't have the right
to not be polite.
And besides, just what is your biz?"

But Alice had no time to answer
for just then a talented dancer
sprang onto the floor,
then leaped out the door,
but let in a calm necromancer.

This "necro" would talk to the dead
whom clearly he heard in his head.
But others could not
even make out the plot,
since they heard only what "necro" said.

A crocodile back from the dead,
was whispering something, he said,
about flowers that talked
and fishes that walked
on their fins when they got out of bed.

"No, this is impossibly crazy,"
said Alice, her mind growing hazy,

"It's time to wake up,
and yes to take up
my chores and to stop being lazy."

And with that our Alice awoke
in a room that was filled with pink smoke:
that seemed a bit strange
but life's about change,
and at least she was back in her poke.

Ode to the semicolon;

a semicolon is a wondrous thing,
a little touch of magic;
you can put; it anywhere you like —
; but to do without it would; be tragic!;
a semicolon is like Superman;
leaping over long sentences in a single; bound —
more powerful than a speeding comma,
knocking periods to the ground
what use have we of question marks;
when the mighty semicolon is on hand;
it is immortal; and omnipotent
accomplishing whatever you have planned;

Look; up in the sky;
it's a bird it's a plane it's a semicolon;
yes, it's a semicolon; strange visitor from another dimension,
that came to the English language
with powers and abilities far beyond
those of ordinary punctuation;
that can change the meaning of otherwise sensible sentences, and which;
disguised as itself;
wages a never-ending battle
to sow ambiguity; and confusion;

https://www.youtube.com/watch?v=BICE9leH0gM&t=62s

ORDINARY LIFE

The whole world's an ashtray

(May be sung to the tune of "St. James' Infirmary")

The whole world's an ashtray
I spread my ash around,
I stick my butt into the ground
Man, that sure feels good.

When I chew gum and when I'm done
I spit it on the street
And when there's gum between my feet,
Man, that sure feels neat.

And when I feel saliva
buildin' up inside my mouth,
I know there's one solution:
gotta gotta spit it out.

The whole world's an ashtray –
cigarette butts and gum and spit,
and when you stop and think about it,
Man, that sure feels good.

Building without mold

So you wanted a building that has no mold –
well, this is something we should have been told
'cause our standard contract is written very plain,
that we're entitled to build in the rain.
And that means mold inside your walls,
insidious slime that creeps and crawls,
puffy fungus that blows in the air,
little mold spores that get in your hair.
If that's not something you were inclined
to want to see, you shouldn't have signed
our standard contract – no, no, no!
you should have requested something apropos.

For triple the price we guarantee
to use materials of high quali-tée
rather than the flimsy cardboard fill
you get with the standard contract quadrille.
For triple the price we'll really try
to do some building when it's dry,
and Mr. Mold will also suffer
if we use our special anti-mold buffer.
But pay attention, please take note
and here I need to read a quote:
right in the special contract read,
"Workers may take the vacation they need."
So yes, we promise that we'll try
to work construction when it's dry,
but that's just if we're not away
soaking up the sun in old Calais.

But we offer a super-special contract too
in which we pledge the entire crew
will give priority to your need
and that our vacations don't supersede:
For six times the posted price you get
a mold-free building with nothing wet.
If that's what you want, let's be precise,
say what you want and pay our price.
We're sorry of course that many of you
have gotten sick with a fungus-flu,
but in the fine print it specifies
we're not responsible if anyone dies –
'cause you wanted mold – that's clear to us,
So we don't see why you raise a fuss.
But good, let's tear the building down
and start afresh with something sound,
we're sure you will be satisfied.
So let's get serious, you decide.

Utensils

The fork met the knife
and said please be my wife,
and let us get married in church
but knife fancied the spoon
and they made honeymoon
and left the fork out in the lurch.

Something in my nose

What have I here inside my nose?
It's something nice, I do suppose,
I shouldn't let it go to waste,
And so I take a little taste!

Derry down down down derry down

(Inspired by George Stevens' 1775 song "What a court hath old England," to the melody of which this verse may be sung.)

I'm worried that I may be coming in late,
I'm worried lest I arrive rather too soon,
I'm worried I may be too formal in dress,
And I'm worried I may be too casually dressed.
Derry down down down derry down,
Derry down down down derry down.

I'm worried the planet is getting too hot,
Maybe I'm ready but maybe I'm not,
I'm worried the planet is getting too cold
And I'm worried that all of my friends look so old.
Derry down down down derry down
Derry down down down derry down.

I'm worried that all of my friends look so young
I'm worried I might have a wart on my tongue,
I'm worried that some of my friends whom I've known
May worry too little or worry alone.
Derry down down down derry down
Derry down down down derry down.

I'm worried the rich control too much wealth,
I'm worried that worrying may harm my health,
It might have effects that are nasty and rough,
and I'm worried that I may not worry enough.
Derry down down down derry down,
Derry down down down derry down.

Where is my wandering robot now?

(For Francine, Richard, and Danielle; may be sung to the tune of "Where is my wandering boy tonight," music composed by Robert Lowry, 1877)

Where is my wandering robot now?
Where is my wandering robot now?
Out out out out
Out on a date with the bread.

All the instructions I carefully read
I told the robot to take out the bread
So the robot took the bread out on a date
and they stayed out ever so late.

Where is my wandering robot now?
Where is my wandering robot now?
Out out out out
Out on a date with the bread.

I know a robot's a thing that is grand
though it is clear that it won't understand
orders that are not totally clear
that's why it acted so queer.

Where is my wandering robot now?
Where is my wandering robot now?
Out out out out
Out on a date with the bread.

Next time I tell the 'bot "clean up this place"
I'll take some care that it does not efface
all of the traces of where we have dwelled
and all the memories we've held.

Where is my wandering robot now?
Where is my wandering robot now?
Out out out out
Out on a date with the bread.

Pizza crisis

(Dedicated to the memory of Bob Hassenstab)

In the telling, in the eating
of a pizza, taste is fleeting
and the taste is best or better
if the cheese is jack or cheddar.

It was a dark and stormy noon,
he ate his pizza with a spoon
tomatoes, mushrooms, onions – fine
but what's this green stuff from the brine?
Origami – now did you say?
with colored paper for your play?
No – I hear it loud and clear –
it's something that won't go with beer.

In the telling, in the eating
of a pizza, taste is fleeting
and the taste is best or better
if the cheese is jack or cheddar.

It was a dark and stormy meal
for it was not the usual deal:
oregano had infiltrated
where all needs had just been sated.
Time for crisis and discussion,
this greenish spice had repercussions,
Down with all these foreign spices!
Welcome to the pizza crisis!

In the telling, in the eating
of a pizza, taste is fleeting
and the taste is best or better
if the cheese is jack or cheddar.

It was a dark and stormy pizza pie –
the kind that makes you groan and sigh,
two little boxes that contained
these greenish flakes of moisture drained,
and parmesan – what's that? – a plot?
What next? Red pepper? Sounds too hot!
In Minnesota, this, our land,
give us liberty and give us bland.

In the telling, in the eating
of a pizza, taste is fleeting
and the taste is best or better
if the cheese is jack or cheddar.

Naked Airlines

(May be sung to the tune of "Mein lieber Herr", from the film "Cabaret" [1972], music by John Kander)

You've booked with Naked Air,
you know you'll travel bare,
we don't allow your clothes on this airline.

We're gonna strap you down,
so come on smile, don't frown,
and you will find this method is fine.

We also have some first-class seating free for you,
but all the first-class passengers are naked too.
We'll shackle both your hands and both your feet as well,
But you'll see, as we tell, that it's swell.

Each seat's a toilet too,
so if you need the loo,
you'll never have to wait in a queue.

We know your safety counts –
that's why we must announce
that carry-ons don't come on this plane.

You know we are the safest airline you can find,
at last you have an airline where you can unwind.
The stewardess will come and feed you like a child:
so relax, it's so safe, nice and mild, nothing wild,
Naked Air, travel bare.

Porridge in tins

Female customer: I want to buy a tin of porridge.

Male attendant: Sorry. We don't sell porridge in tins, only in boxes.

Female customer: No, I want it in a tin. The customer's always right. So, sell me a tin of porridge.

Male attendant: Listen, crazy person, there are no tins of porridge anywhere in the world. You'll have to settle for porridge in a box, or a tin of something else.

Female customer: Porridge should always be sold in a tin,
packing the flavor and keeping it in.
Then you can warm it up right on your stove,
enjoy it for breakfast at home in your cove.
If you don't like it, you throw it away,
horses will eat it and happily bray.
And if you like it, the label you peal
and take to this shop for a good porridge deal.

Male attendant: If there were porridge in tins on the shelf,
I'd surely have seen them, since I am myself
in charge of this shop and everything in it,
so I am the boss and that's how I spin it.
But if you want porridge to feed to your horses,
along with some other delectable courses,
perhaps you can tell me why tins really matter,
or are you so crazy and mad as a hatter?

Female customer: If you won't sell me some porridge in tins,
you probably won't sell me horses with fins
to swim in the pond by the lake near the stream,
though that is the vision I had in a dream.
But maybe you'll sell me some porridge in sacks,
your shop clerks can carry them out on their backs
and bring them to me in my humble abode:
just watch for the posting, "Beware of the toad!"

Father Christmas and Mr. Holly

(When I was living in London as a youngster, my mother would take me just before Christmas to Selfridges on Oxford Street, a prominent department store in downtown London, to visit with Father Christmas, who would hold court in that establishment during Yuletide. There was always a little adventure involved, such as a ride on a "submarine", where the children would sit in rows, while bubbles would be blown on the other side of fake portholes. Then, before we could meet with Father Christmas, we had a chance to talk with his friend, Mr. Holly, a fine gentleman who was always attired entirely in green. This verse, composed in tribute to those delightful experiences of my childhood, may be sung to the tune of "God rest ye merry gentlemen")

Old Father Christmas has a friend, I've seen him in the shop.
His name is Mr. Holly and he used to be a cop,
but now he dresses all in green and dances til he drops,
oh tidings of gladness and zen, gladness and zen,
oh yes, these two are very happy men.

In Selfridges, the mezzanine, these two men have their stead,
Mr. Holly cooks their meals, while St. Nick makes the bed,
and every Friday afternoon the two men bake some bread.
oh tidings of flour and of yeast, flour and yeast,
yes, it's time to plan another Christmas feast!

But then one day Americans claimed that they had found
Father Christmas' long-lost wife, wandering around.
Mrs. Claus, she called herself, but who was Mr. Claus?
oh Mr. Holly got concerned and even rather depressed,
oh tidings of worries from the West.

But Father Christmas reassured his life-long friend and said,
he didn't know this "Mrs. Claus" and never'd shared his bed
with her or any of her friends and rather would be dead,

than to lose what the two-oo men had shared, two men had shared,
and old Mr. Holly shouldn't have despaired.

This "Mrs. Claus" has gone away and lives in Redwood Falls,
she's found a Minnesotan man, a handsome man and tall.
On weekends they just walk around the city's shopping malls.
oh tidings of shopping at the malls, shopping at malls,
then at bowling alleys, rolling down some balls.

Old Father Christmas has a friend, I've seen him in the shop.
His name is Mr. Holly and he used to be a cop,
but now he dresses all in green and dances til he drops,
oh tidings of gladness and zen, gladness and zen,
oh yes, these two are very happy men.

Sayings, or The Adventures of Mick and Butch, Part Two

(Parts One, Three, and Four were published in Is the Moon the Center of the Universe?)

You can't make an omelette without breaking legs.
Mick wanted some breakfast, so he knee-capped Butch.
Every shroud has a silver lining –
which explains why Butch stole shrouds.
The Mass is always meaner on the other side –
which explains why Mick did not convert to Satanism.
You can lead a hearse to the water, but you cannot make it sink:
Butch had a different opinion, and sank the hearse, with Mick's body in it.
Where there's a will, there's an inheritance;
unfortunately for Butch, Mick had not left him anything.

Gourmette cuisine (oh, you wanted gourmet dining?)

(For Mikhail Gradovski.)

So you're wanting quesadilla –
that's a treat for you and me-ya.
Here's the way we make it here,
bet your mouth is watering, dear:
Fried tortilla, finger-lickin',
just add lettuce and some chicken,
half a teaspoon grated cheese,
sliced tomato if you please,
thousand island, what a treat!
Now it's ready, time to eat!

Chicken Kiev's so delicious,
and our recipe's ambitious.
We're proud our take is quite original,
using only foods indiginal.
Vodka floating on your plate,
lettuce that we'll rehydrate,
chicken and some grated cheese,
sliced tomato if you please,
thousand island, what a treat!
Now it's ready, time to eat!

Tacos? Yes, we serve that too:
big demand, get in the queue.
Our chief is such a cooking master,
was a time he was a pastor.
Some jalapenos start the brew,
bed of lettuce, chicken too,
sliced tomato if you please,

and a little grated cheese,
thousand island, what a treat!
Now it's ready, time to eat!

T-bone steak? Why that's our specialty,
and we make it nice and freshalty.
We're sure that you'll be quite awe-stricken
when you learn we're using chicken.
Sprinkle parsley all around,
lettuce, chicken – half a pound,
half a teaspoon grated cheese,
sliced tomato if you please,
thousand island, what a treat!
Now it's ready, time to eat!

My father told me

(For Fiona, Sophus, and Olav)

My father told me whales can speak,
but in fact just once a week.
My father told me lizards fly,
they sprout their wings, take to the sky.
My father told me pirates sing,
explicating everything.
My father told me I'll be queen,
my gown will have a silvery sheen.
My father told me that great deeds
are written down in books I read.
My father gave me seven pounds
and sent me out for coffee grounds.

Yeah, happy brush!

A maiden on the misty heath
showing off her listy teeth,
An arc of triumph, crown of gold
fitted as an alginate mold.
Behold the mighty tube of paste,
with its apple-mango taste!
A brushing here, a brushing there
and there'll be no cavities anywhere!
Yeah, happy brush, none can withstand
your application by my hand.
Bacteria tremble, quake in fear
when my toothbrush draweth near.
Hail, toothbrush! I love your feel --
that's why I use you after every meal.

Shampoo causes insanity

Shampoo causes insanity – it soaks into your brain,
my neighbor uses shampoo daily, and now he's quite insane.
But you need to wash your hair – so try a little salt.
Those who wash their hair this way might just end up bald,
but find a single salter who's completely lost all sense:
no! you cannot do it, not even one who's dense.

My neighbor worships my dog

Tim my neighbor's big and burly,
was a cop, retired early,
misses chases with his siren,
bought a toy and did some wirin'.
Bought himself an ice-cream van,
then proceeded with his plan:
turns his makeshift siren on,
has his water pistol drawn,
flashing lights both green and yellow,
and on his megaphone he bellows:
"THIS IS NOT THE POLICE.
DO NOT PULL OVER TO THE SIDE OF THE ROAD.
REPEAT: THIS IS NOT THE POLICE.
DO NOT PULL OVER TO THE SIDE OF THE ROAD."

Tim has a dog but prefers mine,
he thinks that my pooch is divine.
Every night I hear him praying
and with his hymns he is conveying
joyous signs of adulation
for our doggie (a Dalmatian).
What he wants is reinstatement
in the force – there's no abatement
in his litany for help,
but my doggie, who's no whelp,
ignores his prayers and his pleas –
he's busy brushing off some fleas.

I'm worried 'bout my neighbor, Tim,
but I'm not sure what to do for him:
meanwhile Tim continues odd,
worshipping my pooch as God.

A guide on how to riot

So you want to riot – well, here's a little guide:
if you want to riot, it's got to be outside.
If you stay inside your bedroom – here's a little clue –
it doesn't count as rioting, no matter what you do.
You can throw around the pillows and overturn the bed,
even shoot a round of bullets through a loaf of bread.
You can blame your little teddy bear for your current woe,
but none of this is rioting – believe me, as I know.

You've got to do some shouting, slogans and the like,
and always do some running: you're not just on a hike.
Banners are essential, hoist them to the sky,
and drink some alcohol before, to help you think you're high.
But most important – this I know – it likely would be best
to wear a metal helmet and a bullet-proof vest.
Now you're ready, grab your banner, go out on the street,
shout and curse and run a bit, on your dancing feet.

Rabbit Hood

(Constructed on the template of the introduction to "The Adventures of Robin Hood", a British television series, starring Richard Greene, which aired from 1955 to 1960)

He called his clan of rabbits
to a nearby rabbit patch,
they vowed to keep their lettuce clean and fresh.
They chased away the insects
that were threatening their stash,
and still found plenty of time to sing:
"Rabbit Hood, Rabbit Hood, carrot in his hand.
Rabbit Hood, Rabbit Hood – no food that is canned.
Feared by the bugs, loved by the hares,
Rabbit Hood, Rabbit Hood, Rabbit Hood."

The Lone Rabbit

(This verse is built, in part, on the template of the introduction to "The Lone Ranger", a television series which starred Clayton Moore as the Lone Ranger, and ran from 1949 to 1957)

The Lone Rabbit to the rescue!
A fiery rabbit with the speed of light, a cloud of dust,
and a hearty "Hi ho, carrots!"
The Lone Rabbit rides again!
With his trusty side-kick, Wadley the Weasel,
this artistic rabbit sets down his easel,
whenever a damsel or fellow's in distress,
whenever there's need to clean up some mess,
rounding up looters and rotten polluters:
The Lone Rabbit rides again!

Yo-ho yo, a professor's life for me

(With thanks to song writers for the ride at "Disneyland" in Anaheim, where the song "Yo-ho, yo-ho, a pirate's life for me" was first performed for the public. The entire ride, complete with singing, is posted at
https://www.youtube.com/watch?v=Uv7APUxrebw)

Yo-ho yo, a professor's life for me,
we teach, we read, we write, we think, we're working through the night
and other people read our work
and then they tell us we're right!

Yo-ho yo, a professor's life for me
our students always come to class, they read assignments twice
and when they sit for their exams
their answers more than suffice!

Yo-ho yo, a professor's life for me
I read a book the other day that's full of lively thoughts,
I think I'll let those thoughts sink in
while sailing around on my yacht.

Yo-ho, yo-ho, yo-ho ho!

Thick rubber membrane

(Originally published under the title "I just can't help myself")

Thick rubber membrane, sitting on the roof,
cuddly little doggies going "woof woof!"
I'm sitting on my rocker, staring at the clouds,
Watching people I didn't like lying under shrouds.
I just can't help myself, I think I need some okra,
While I sit and wait, I drink a little mocca.
78 rpm's are spinning round and round,
While I'm here I'm resting somewhere near the ground.
Thick rubber membrane, sitting on the roof,
cuddly little doggies going "woof woof!"
Sometimes I imagine I'm living on the moon,
as far as I'm aware, there's still a lot of room.
Rents are low, crime is low, but dating is a problem,
Not so many girls and boys, not even just a goblin.
I just can't help myself, I've got to give a speech,
there are a ton of lessons I'm ready now to teach.
People need instruction, and I am qualified,
to tell them what they're doing wrong, and how their brains are fried.
Thick rubber membrane, sitting on the roof,
cuddly little doggies going "woof woof!"

MENTAL, DENTAL, & PHYSICAL HEALTH

Colonoscopy

(The metrical scheme is inspired by "Dixie", a song written by Daniel Decatur Emmett of Mt. Vernon, Ohio, and premiered in New York in September 1859. It was later much loved in the doomed Confederacy, where it was adopted as the de facto anthem)

When the doctor comes with his big syringe
I wince and whimper and I cringe
and look away, look away, look away at the floor.

He draws some liquid, gives a squirt
and tells me that the jab won't hurt.
I look away, look away, look away at the door.

I don't think I'm a cynic, Hooray! Hooray!
but I don't like it being here,
visiting the clinic.
Away, away, please let me out the doorway!
Away, away, please let me out the doorway!

He's sending something up my anus,
and the pain is tough and heinous,
look away, look away, look away at the floor.

The doctor tells me the pain is nascent
and says that I'm a charming patient,
but look away, look away, look away at the door.

I'm not sure he's a doctor, Hooray! Hooray!
Don't you think we ought to have
someone here to proctor,
to check, to check, to make sure he's a doctor,
Away, away, please let me out the doorway.
Away, away, please let me out the doorway!

Song of the happy brain surgeons

We've come to an assessment that you're partly insane,
we're taking out our scalpels and we're fixing your brain.
Just settle back, don't worry, know that you're in good hands,
with every error that we make our knowledge expands.
And when you wake tomorrow you'll feel happy and fresh,
forget about your troubles now and banish all stress.
It's only every now and then that something goes wrong,
and sometimes it's because we are all singing a song.
The other day a patient had an ache in his head,
rather than prescribing pills what we did instead --
lobotomy was what we did, but when it was done,
the patient didn't have complaints and thought it all was fun.
We get distracted all the time -- for that there's no cure;
though concentrating's hard, all our intentions are pure.
And if a brain falls on the floor, we know that it will bounce,
we like our job, we're having fun, and that is all that counts.

There's a rabbit in my brain

Hey doctor doctor doctor
there's a rabbit in my brain
hey doctor doctor doctor
he's driving me insane
hey doctor doctor doctor
he's talking all day long
hey doctor doctor doctor
I think there's something wrong.

Can you give me drugs to fix me up?
(now) that would be so swell
You gotta have a tablet that will work
to get me feelin' well.
Maybe there's a pill that I can take
to shut this rabbit up
He's talkin' lotsa nonsense all the time
I'm ready to give up.

Hey doctor doctor doctor
there's a rabbit in my brain
hey doctor doctor doctor
he's driving me insane
hey doctor doctor doctor
he's talking all day long
hey doctor doctor doctor
I think there's something wrong.

He's chattering away without a break
it's more than I can take,
he offers his opinions constantly –
he makes my whole brain ache.
Can you give me shots to tranquilize
this rabbit in my head?
Maybe if I take some sleeping pills,
the hare will go to bed.

Hey doctor doctor doc-doc
there's a rabbit in my brain
hey doctor doctor doctor
he's driving me insane
hey doctor doctor doctor
he's talking all day long
hey doctor doctor doctor
I think there's something wrong.

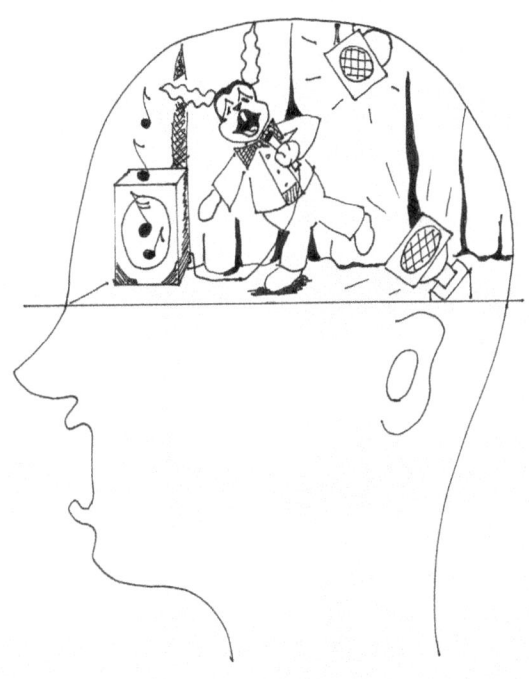

The secret of long life

(To be sung to the melody of "16 tons," a song popularized by Tennessee Ernie Ford, but also performed by Johnny Cash, Willie Nelson, and Tom Jones, among others)

Some people say a man oughta drink alcohol,
Wine every day makes you healthy and whole,
It relaxes your body and sharpens your mind,
And quality wine is easy to find.

Old Jake Pickens thought what he'd been told,
Was the Gospel truth til the day he grew old.
Wine bottles in the kitchen, and he was sure,
That he owed his life to wine as a cure.

Other people say that alcohol's bad,
Better to avoid it, lest it drive you mad,
It hurts your liver and dulls your brain,
Before you know it, you are half insane.

Old Suzie Mae agreed with all that,
Never drank spirits or wine from the vat,
When she reached the age of a hundred and two,
The reason, she thought, was her milk-shake brew.

Still other folk "know" you should get lotsa sleep,
Just like on your back and count the sheep.
The longer you doze, the longer you live,
This is th'advice that some folks give.

Ole Billy Bob spent his life in bed,
Scarcely got up til the day he was dead.
When he reached the age of a hundred and four,
The reason he thought was "sleep and snore".

Ya know it's gotta be that others disagree,
Too much sleep robs your energy.
It destroys your muscles and erases your mind,
You don't need to sleep just to unwind.

Old Debbie Daisy didn't like to snooze,
She skipped the colas and she skipped the booze.
She stayed awake til a hundred and one,
And by staying awake, she had more fun,
And by staying awake, she had more fun.

O Tannlege

(Composed in December 2013, in Norwegian, with translation following; to the tune of "O Tannenbaum")

O Tannlege, O Tannlege, så deilig er bedøvelsen.
Jeg liker ikke smerten min, jeg liker metallboren din.
O Tannlege, O Tannlege, så deilig er bedøvelsen.

O Tannlege, O Tannlege, så vakkert er kontoret ditt.
Ja, bordet ditt er veldig rent og spyttekumet – veldig pent.
O Tannlege, O Tannlege, så vakkert er kontoret ditt.

Oh Dentist, Oh Dentist, your anaesthetic is so delicious.
I don't like my pain, I like your metal drill.
Oh Dentist, Oh Dentist, your anaesthetic is so delicious.

Oh Dentist, Oh Dentist, your office is so beautiful.
Your table, yes, is very clean and your spit basin – very pretty.
Oh Dentist, Oh Dentist, your office is so beautiful.

Dental work in Tijuana (another Christmas song, of sorts)

(This verse should be sung to the tune of "White Christmas," melody by Irving Berlin. Dedicated to JR, who loves Christmas songs)

I've never been to Tijuana –
no, never ever in my life.
Well, OK, maybe, when I had rabies,
I may have been there once or twice.

I'm dreaming of a low-cost dentist,
with every cavity I get.
May your teeth be merry and white,
and may all your dental work delight.

You'll find the dentists there work cheaply,
at least the ones that don't pay tax.
If your teeth need fixing, the drinks are mixing,
just take a swig and then relax.

I've booked my flight to Tijuana,
I will be seated in the aisle.
In th'event we crash on our route,
my clean teeth will give me cause to smile.

Haircuts in Honolulu

I often travel to Hawaii, but never while awake,
I sleep, I dream, I dream some more, and then I take a break:
I'm flying to Hawaii on my Big Dog motorbike,
Coco Palms is where I land, and then I grab the mike.
I'm singing now, the crowd goes wild, they stomp their feet and cheer,
the owners are so happy, 'cause the people want more beer.
I've come to see the wildlife, the Hoary Bat no less,
but I end up in a barber shop, with my hair in quite a mess.
The barber stands there, smiles at me but always looking formal,
Says to me, "Just take a seat. Hello! I'm very normal.
Here's a coffee, sugar too, for gustatory sipping,
wait your turn, it's coming soon, and then we'll start some clipping."
I have this dream so often and I always hope to see,
some exotic flowers, wildlife, and beaches by the sea.
But every time I dream this dream, I see a distant harbor,
but head downtown and find myself once more with the barber.
This dream seems surrealistic and even paranormal,
But the barber simply greets me: "Hello! I'm very normal.
Here's a coffee, sugar too, for gustatory sipping,
wait your turn, it's coming soon, and then we'll start some snipping."
I try to tell the barber that he cut my hair last week,
but he nods so very sweetly and does not want to speak.
I try to find a therapist, but only in my dreams,
I don't need one in actual life, it's only what it seems.
But try to poke 'round Honolulu in a dreaming state,
You find an office, verify the name that's on the plate.
Therapy, the nameplate claims, but once you are inside,
You're looking at a barber, who's looking satisfied.

The barber stands there, smiles at me but always looking formal,
and then he simply greets me: "Hello! I'm very normal.
Here's a coffee, sugar too, for gustatory sipping,
wait your turn, it's coming soon, and then we'll start some clipping."

Should I be concerned?

My youngest child's first words were "Comrade Stalin" –
should I be concerned?
My dog has false teeth, but I have no idea how he got them –
should I be concerned?
My therapist has had a lobotomy –
should I be concerned?
All my neighbors had plastic surgery so that they could look just like me –
should I be concerned?
My spouse wants us to take our next vacation in the Bermuda triangle –
should I be concerned?

OUTER SPACES, LOCAL BASES, FOREIGN PLACES

Best toilets in the galaxy

We've come from Planet Zoot
we wear a special suit
and we don't want to soil it
so take us to your toilet.

We're from a distant star
we've traveled very far
so please please understand
why we've had to land.

Around the galax-ee
when someone has to pee
we're always satisfied
with toilets we have tried

that you have right here
on earth, aquatic sphere.
So, take us to your leader?
But do we need to meet her?

Must she give permission
for a fast emission?
We don't want to soil it,
please take us to your toilet.

There's pressure on the bladder
and yes we'll feel much gladder,
and once we can relax
we'll thank you to the max!

Alien implant

One night as I was sleeping some aliens dropped in,
they landed on the rooftop and then they all popped in.
They slid on down our chimney and took a look around,
they all looked like Omar Sharif with both feet on the ground.
They grabbed my little finger and put an implant in,
they said it was a souvenir, I think it's made of tin.
I don't know what it's for, or why they came to me,
but somehow I am certain that this implant is the key
to understanding what they want and why they left so quickly,
and why not even one of them was looking pale or sickly.
I like my little implant, I take it everywhere,
you shouldn't look at me that way, you know it's rude to stare.

Home, sweet home

Whenever I'm on Jupiter I always throw a fit,
because they don't have chairs up there: where is a chump to sit?

Now when I visit Pluto, to attend a research meeting,
I'm often feeling very cold: you'd think they'd have some heating!

Then, if you write a letter home, you'll find that on Uranus,
there's no place where you can post it: for that, the planet's famous.

And is there life on Saturn's rings? Man, you must be joking!
The routine there is deadly dull: I find it really choking.

But Mercury's the oddest because it's not rotating.
You've got to choose – it's day or dark: I find it so frustrating.

And so when I consider where else that I could move,
I think that Earth's the best around: I fit right in the groove.

Forward, brothers!

Forward, brothers! We will win:
if we don't, we'll lose ag'in.
Everyone should think like us,
if they don't, we'll make a fuss.
We'll commit mass suicide
if the people won't decide
that we brothers know what's right:
right is right, and might makes might.

Oh, sociology, don't you cry for me

(Dedicated to Kristen Ringdal and Al Simkus)

I read a book the other night when everything was pure,
it might have been Max Weber, though I'm no longer sure.
Or maybe it was Parsons, but I already forgot –
I know I read some socio, I just can't tell you what.

Oh, sociology, don't you cry for me,
'cause I have Emile Durkheim's book sitting on my knee.

Whenever I read Aron, it always drive me wild:
he must have been so brilliant already as a child.
And when I read some Pierre Bourdieu it always makes me cry,
but truly, for the life of me, I really don't know why.

Oh, sociology, don't you cry for me,
'cause I have Emile Durkheim's book sitting on my knee.

Welcome in our hotel!

Welcome in our hotel, guest dearest!
Happiness can be yours
at the flick of the wrist.
Just call our wish-fulfillment table
and reserve your needs.
Breakfast on bed at your pleasure,
wine in your mouth
in our wine-dipping lounge,
and don't forget dinner:
inspired by our chef, now resting.
Have it your way
with our conference center,
equipped fully with microphones
and chairs.
And if you want relaxing
at end of work all day,
a soothing massage waits for you
in the hotel's "soft touch" massage parlor.
Yes, guest dearest, happiness can be yours!
Check-out time is unfortunately noon daily.

Bring back my Bonnie to me – zombie version

(May be sung to the tune of "My Bonnie lies over the ocean," a traditional Scottish folk song)

My Bonnie was buried last Tuesday
her coffin lies under a mound
but some folks can dig up your loved ones
and bring them back out of the ground.

Bring back, bring back, oh bring back my Bonnie to me, to me,
Bring back, bring back, oh bring back my Bonnie to me.

I know that she might be a zombie
her brain will no longer be right,
she's scratchin' away at the coffin,
once out she will look quite a fright.

Bring back, bring back, oh bring back my Bonnie to me, to me,
Bring back, bring back, oh bring back my Bonnie to me.

Oh come on guys, help with the shovel,
please dig away some of the dirt,
my zombie-girl may still be breathing,
I'm sure that she's not yet inert.

Bring back, bring back, oh bring back my Bonnie to me, to me,
Bring back, bring back, oh bring back my Bonnie to me.

I'm gonna sail to Liechtenstein

(This verse is set to the meter of "Camptown Races," a song composed by Stephen Collins Foster, 1826-1864)

I'm gonna sail to Liechtenstein, doo-dah, doo-dah!
I know there's neither sea nor brine, oh doo-dah day!
Oh doo-dah day, oh doo-dah day,
I'm gonna sail to Liechtenstein, oh doo-dah day!

I'm settin' sail from Budapest, doo-dah, doo-dah!
I think I know the route that's best, oh doo-dah day!
Oh doo-dah day, oh doo-dah day!
I'm settin' sail from Budapest, oh doo-dah day!

So, load my ship on a flatbed truck, doo-dah, doo-dah!
I'm counting on my usual luck, oh doo-dah day!
Oh doo-dah day, oh doo-dah day!
So, load my ship on a flatbed truck, oh doo-dah day!

I know the driver knows the way, doo-dah, doo-dah!
It's effortless to sail this way, oh doo-dah day!
Oh doo-dah day, oh doo-.dah day!
It's effortless to sail this way, oh doo-dah day!

Hotel Gabrovo
(International Joke Capital of the World, and of Europe)

(For Thomas Berker)

Welcome here in our hotel,
where our pleasures can be your pleasures.
We are proud to announce, darling guests,
that our hotel has not been attacked by terrorists
since 2008.
Rooms all equipped with beds and lamps.
Desks and chairs available on request.
Toilet down the hall, as well as bath.
Telephone service Mondays through Fridays:
weekends are off for telephone operator —
as she deserves, you will agree, guest darling.
No television in room,
but live entertainment in your room upon request.
We regret that dead entertainer was found in room 23
some years back,
but he has since been fired and corpse removed,
along with day manager.
OK, it happened once — but nothing happened,
since he was already dead.
Check out the indoor/outdoor training center
on fifth floor, complete with simulated bus.
Swimming pool very convenient —
an easy 20-minute bus ride
on mostly paved road.
Snakes along road? no worry:
we shoot them for you.
Elevators have been reinforced and electrified
for your safety.

Staircase upgraded, also new manager.
Throw towels on floor, we clean up —
or think of not wasting our water.
When leaving, give positive feedback:
last year, feedback was negative,
and entire staff was dismissed.
Good for us — we have new jobs!
Welcome in our hotel!

The Earth is a spaceship

The earth is a spaceship but what about Mars?
We know it's a planet up high with the stars.
The one with the ring, the one we call Saturn –
also a planet, thus fitting the pattern.
Venus and Neptune, Uranus too,
are planets, not spaceships and lovely to view.
But Pluto's no planet, or so we've been told –
it might be a spaceship, made of copper and gold.
And if it's a spaceship, it must have some creatures
building ice castles on the spaceship's cool beaches.
There's no global warming on Pluto, it seems:
it could be our back-up, the home of our dreams.
But how shall we get there? I'm glad you asked:
we live on a spaceship, the crew can be tasked
to get us there safely with all that we'll need
on Pluto, the spaceship: that is my creed.

About the Author

Sabrina P. Ramet is a Professor Emerita at the Norwegian University of Science and Technology in Trondheim. She is the author of 14 scholarly books and two novels, both published by Scarith Books: *Café Bombshell: The International Brain Surgery Conspiracy* (2008) and *The Curse of the Aztec Dummy: A Nebraskan Chronicle* (2017).

About the Illustrator

Christine M. Hassenstab, who prepared the artwork for this volume, earned her Ph.D. in sociology at the Norwegian University of Science and Technology in 2010. She was a public defender in a previous life. She and Sabrina have a cat named Jascha, a calm and unusually friendly cat.

www.ingramcontent.com/pod-product-compliance
Lightning Source LLC
Chambersburg PA
CBHW051057160426
43193CB00010B/1223